Why Do Bees Buzz?

Animal Q&A: Fascinating Answers to Questions about Animals

Animal Q&A books invite readers to explore the secret lives of animals. Covering everything from their basic biology to their complex behaviors at every stage of life to issues in conservation, these richly illustrated books provide detailed information in an accessible style that brings to life the science and natural history of a variety of species.

Do Butterflies Bite? Fascinating Answers to Questions about Butterflies and Moths, by Hazel Davies and Carol A. Butler

Do Bats Drink Blood? Fascinating Answers to Questions about Bats, by Barbara A. Schmidt-French and Carol A. Butler

Why Do Bees Buzz?

*Fascinating Answers
to Questions about Bees*

Elizabeth Capaldi Evans
and Carol A. Butler

Rutgers University Press
NEW BRUNSWICK, NEW JERSEY, AND LONDON

Library of Congress Cataloging-in-Publication Data

Evans, Elizabeth Capaldi, 1968–
    Why do bees buzz? : fascinating answers to questions about bees /
Elizabeth Capaldi Evans and Carol A. Butler.
        p. cm. — (Animal Q & A)
    Includes bibliographical references and index.
    ISBN 978-0-8135-4721-3 (pbk. : alk. paper)
        1. Bees—Miscellanea. I. Butler, Carol A., 1943– II. Title.
QL563.E88 2010
595.79'9—dc22
                                                    2009027621

A British Cataloging-in-Publication record for this book is available
from the British Library.

Visit our Web site: http://rutgerspress.rutgers.edu

Manufactured in the United States of America

Contents

A color insert follows page   112

Preface

Written by Carol A. Butler, the co-author of *Do Butterflies Bite?*, along with bee biologist Elizabeth Capaldi Evans, this book is the only guide to these popular insects to present information in an accessible and entertaining question-and-answer format. We touch everything from the role bees play in the ecosystem to their amazing variety, what life in the bee colony is like, and the crisis of their disappearance. We also provide useful information about how to observe bees safely and how to raise bees in your backyard. Photographs and illustrations add to the beauty and usefulness of the book.

We have tried to put together a fascinating set of questions about bee behavior, bee lore, and beekeeping. Here are some of the surprising facts about bees you will discover in the book:

- There are about 25,000 different species of bees around the world.
- It is normal for a honey bee queen to lay from 1,500 to 2,000 eggs in one day.
- Bees are the only insects for which artificial insemination techniques have been successfully developed.
- Most honey bees only live for a few weeks.

We hope you enjoy this book and use it in any way that suits you best. Look up an answer to a question that you have been curious about, browse through randomly, or just look at the illustrations for a start. There is a lot in this book, and we would not be surprised if you get hooked and find yourself reading it all the way through and, hopefully, sharing your new insights with friends and family.

Acknowledgments

From Elizabeth: Fortune has favored me with a fantastic family that fostered my love of the natural world from an early age; their encouragement inspired me to pursue a career in science and education. My thanks go to them for all they have done to support me. My husband, David W. Evans, continues to be a source of joy, friendship, and possibility; I am grateful to share this life with him. Deb Cook-Balducci, information technologist, Kathleen McQuiston, science librarian, and Karen Shrawder and Eileen Spade, administrative assistants, are expert staff members at Bucknell University; they were very helpful in my work on this book. I also appreciate the assistance or advice of Puja Batra, Craig Cella, John Cullum, Julie Dlugos, Jonathan Gelernter, Marie Pizzorno, Gene Robinson, Tom Seeley, and Jeri Wright. Special thanks to the International Bee Research Association for permitting us to use one of their images.

From Carol: Our thanks to Doreen Valentine and the Rutgers team for their support and to Deirdre Mullane for her advice and guidance. Special thanks to Erich Stadler for his persistence in helping us locate Armand Whitehead, so we could get Armand's permission to use his wonderful scanning electron microscopic image of the tip of a bee antennae—it has been my screen saver (courtesy of Erich) while we wrote this book. Our thanks to Adrian Dyer and Susan Miller, who allowed us to use their beautiful images of a flower as seen by a bee, and to Janet David and Elizabeth Johnson of the American Museum of Natural History for their contributions to the discussion of bee research being conducted in New York City. We are grateful to George West for his bee drawings that appear throughout the book. This has been a long road, and I have received a lot of encouragement from friends and family for which I am grateful.

Why Do Bees Buzz?

ONE

Bee Basics

Question 1: What are bees?

Answer: Bees are invertebrate animals that grow through four different life stages—egg, larva, pupa, and adult—similar to the seemingly friendlier insects, the butterflies. However, unlike butterflies, which abandon their eggs once they are laid, bees provide their young a safe place to hatch and grow. All juvenile bees develop within the protected confines of an enclosed nest that is built by a female bee or by other females in the family. In some social species, the bee babies, or larvae, are fed on demand by their sisters. In other bee species, the larvae are enclosed within a small chamber after food has been deposited inside it. While often confused with wasps, their more aggressive, meat-eating cousins, bees almost always collect and feed on nectar and pollen from plants. These food resources may be consumed directly, stored within the nest, or made into provisions for later generations.

Bees and wasps do share a common ancestry, as evidenced by their superficially similar bodies; insects in each group have a "wasp waist"—the narrow area between the thorax (middle body-part) and the abdomen (end body-part). Both types of insects have many hairs on their bodies, but the hairs on bees are fluffy or branched; the hairs on wasps are typically straight and somewhat shiny. Both also have two sets of wings that fold back on top of one another when not in use and hook together during flight, and many species have similar coloration on their bodies

Bees and social wasps, like hornets and yellow jackets, evolved from a common, solitary wasp ancestor that was dependent on other insects as a protein source for its developing larvae. Bees now rely only on pollen as a source of protein for their young. Once bees metamorphose into adults, they do not grow, and adult bees only require fuel for movement and flight. *Nectar*, from the Latin "drink of the gods," is the bees' sugar-rich source of energy, so flowers provide everything the bees need. Other animals, like hummingbirds and many nectivorous bats, must supplement their nectar-drinking with protein from insects in order to sustain their own growth.

Bees are grouped within the insects in the order Hymenoptera, which includes the sawflies, wasps, and ants (see this chapter, question 4: How are bees classified?). Many of the members of this order have a sting that is used to defend the nest. Although bees and wasps are often mistaken for one another, these two types of insects are quite different. First, bees and wasps have different temperaments. While bees are often characterized as aggressive, they are typically docile and harmless, using only their stings when provoked near the hive. Yellow jackets, on the other hand, can be quite aggressive, even when away from the nest. Moreover, it is wasps that are likely to invade your picnic, not bees. Indeed, bees are misunderstood, and their bad reputation is a result of being confused with their more aggressive cousins.

Question 2: What is special about honey bees?

Answer: Honey bees, the focal bees of this book, lead very complex social lives; but most bees live alone, don't make or store honey, and only very rarely sting. Approximately 85 percent of bee species are more or less solitary, although some species make nests close together, sometimes forming huge aggregations. These clusters of individual nests are like a large apartment complex, with many individuals living in a common location, but each making their own way in the world. Some bees are communal, with several females of the same generation sharing a nest, and about one thousand species of bees live in very small, temporary colonies consisting of a queen and a few daughters. These colonies die out when the weather turns cold, and only some pupa, or in some species the queen, survive the winter. During the warm weather months, the resources in the environment are shared, so as different flower species bloom, different bee species are seen for a few weeks and then they seemingly vanish.

Honey bee colonies, in contrast, are huge—often containing over fifty thousand bees—and they are perpetual, continuing on for many years following an annual cycle. The European or Western honey bee, *Apis mellifera*, is the most intensively studied bee species and probably the insect you imagine when you think of a typical bee. They are at home both in natural cavity nests and in artificial hives, and they have a caste system with a queen, workers, and drones. Honey bees are specialized to be efficient pollinators, engaging in behaviors and having physical attributes (pollen baskets on their legs, for example) that are specifically aimed at efficiently gathering nectar and pollen to feed their brood. Given the nickname "pollen pigs" by some afficionados, honey bees are generalists in that they visit an exceptional diversity of plants to acquire food for their family. In the course of their foraging, they incidentally fertilize a wide range of plants, making it possible for the plants to reproduce and bear fruit.

In the winter, when the activity in the honey bee nest slows down to a crawl because there are no flowers to provide nectar supplies, the adult honey bees live for months in a quiescent state. Unlike other social insects like social wasps or bumblebees, they are not hibernators; they consume honey stores and shiver to generate the metabolic heat that allows them to withstand frigid winter temperatures. They become active again when the first flowers begin to bloom, gathering supplies to sustain the future generations in the colony. In the warm weather, each honey bee only lives a few weeks, to be replaced by other adult bees as they reach maturity, and this relay of family members continues as long as the growing season lasts.

Question 3: How many species of bees exist?

Answer: Bees are found almost everywhere, sometimes in surprising places. There are approximately twenty-five thousand species of bees in the world, about thirty-five hundred species in North America, and even in the middle of New York City's Central Park more than sixty species have been identified. Scientists have always distinguished one species from another by observing the details of their mouthparts, wing veins, size, body hair, tongue, and pollen-carrying structures, and by their nesting and foraging behaviors. Now that DNA analysis is available as an additional tool, relationships and differences among species are being further clarified.

Most of the answers in this book describe honey bees because of their long association with people; scientists know more about their behavior than about many other types of bees. Honey bees are a social species, living in large, perennial colonies headed by a queen. They are by far the most economically important bees in the United States. Historically, populations of native bees have been negatively impacted by various land-use practices—this history, as well as the solitary nature of most native species, means that honey bees have become the pollinator of choice for many agricultural crops.

Approximately 85 percent of bees are solitary species, meaning that a single female emerges from her pupal case, mates, and then constructs one or more individual cells that she provisions with nectar and pollen. She may burrow into the ground to make her nest, or she may create a cell in an existing hole in a tree, plant stem, or other material. Then she lays an egg directly on the food supply, and the egg develops into an adult bee that repeats the cycle. When there are limited areas in the habitat that are suitable for nesting, hundreds or even thousands of solitary bees may nest in close proximity. Male solitary bees usually are short-lived, whether they mate once or several times.

Bumblebees (family Bombidae) are native to the United States and are distributed on many other continents as well. Their colo-

Fig. 1. A bumblebee (*Bombus pennsylvanicus*) worker with a filled pollen
basket visible on her hind leg. (*Drawing by Julie L. Dlugos.*)

nies are relatively small. Only the queen survives the winter, and
although she is larger than the female workers (called callows),
her body structure is basically the same as that of the workers.
She needs to forage when the warm weather arrives because she
is the only bee alive in the nest, which differs from the honey
bee queen, who never needs to forage because she is always surrounded by attendants. Although bumblebees forage for pollen
and nectar to feed their young, they make very little honey and
it cannot be harvested by people.

Stingless bees (family Meliponidae) evolved earlier than
honey bees, and they are found in the tropics on every continent, strongly suggesting that they evolved before the continents
separated approximately seventy million years ago. They nest in

Fig. 2. Multiple large colonies (visible as the large dark shapes on the rocks) of *Apis dorsata* adorn this cliff in Biligiri Rangaswamy Temple Wildlife Sanctuary, Karnataka, India. Note the bamboo ladders on the cliff; these ladders are erected by people who work as honey collectors. (*Photograph © Puja Batra.*)

cavities, usually inside a tree trunk or in a branch; some nest inside the nests of other insects, such as ants or termites. For more about stingless bees, see chapter 9, question 1: Do all bees sting? and chapter 9, question 7: How do stingless bees defend themselves?

Giant honey bees (*Apis dorsata* and *Apis laboriosa*) are found in Asia, and they make large nests out in the open that hang from tree branches or rock overhangs. They nest gregariously, with the result that there can be as many as a hundred individual nests in the branches of one tree. Their nests are often depicted in prehistoric rock paintings.

Many solitary species belong to the family Halictidae and are typically called sweat bees because many of them are attracted to the salts in human perspiration. After the halictid female

Fig. 3. A common sweat bee in the genus *Lasioglossum,* a member of the family Halictidae. This bee is approximately 1 cm long. (*Drawing by Julie L. Dlugos.*)

mates, she builds her own small nest in the soil or in a small enclosure within a plant stem, dead tree, or sandy embankment. She gathers pollen and nectar, combines them, deposits a pellet of this paste in each cell and lays an egg on each bit of food. Then she usually dies and her offspring emerge and repeat her pattern. Sweat bees are small and dark colored, often with light-colored bands of hair or a metallic sheen to their body. Some species may help each other and even share a nesting tunnel, but most do not cooperate.

Mining bees (family Andrenidae) are considered "semi-social," characterized by their soil nests with branching chambers. At the end of each chamber are one or more cells. There is some group organization but there is no definite caste system and no queen, and they are less social than sweat bees.

Leafcutter bees (family Megachilidae) have long tongues and carry pollen on their abdominal hairs, known as scopa. Females make thimble-shaped chambers of folded leaves along a tunnel in the ground or in a hollow plant stem, and they accumulate honey and pollen and lay an egg in each chamber. Close relatives of the leafcutter bees are mason bees, which nest in nail holes or other pre-existing cavities in wood. They fill each hole with honey and pollen and then lay an egg in it and cap it with mud. These females can produces one or two eggs per day.

Cellophane bees (family Colletidae), also called plasterer or polyester bees, nest in soil burrows or in twigs and plant stems, depending on the genus. One genus, *Hylaeus*, is relatively hairless and looks somewhat wasp-like. Instead of secreting wax, bees in this family line their brood cells with a secretion that hardens into a cellophane-like membrane.

Carpenter or digger bees (family Apidae) are hairy and fast flying and typically nest in the ground or build a nest in wood. They carry pollen on their legs, and they have long tongues and are excellent pollinators. One common species of carpenter bee in the eastern United States resembles the bumblebee in body size and coloration, but carpenter bees are solitary while bumblebees are social in small colonies that are founded by one queen.

Parasitic bees, which belong to many different families, do not forage for nectar or make their own nests, and they are not equipped to gather pollen. They invade the nests of other bees and lay their eggs in the nests of their hosts. When their larvae emerge, they feed on the stored food that was meant for the host larvae. These parasites may go so far as to kill the eggs or larvae they find in the nest. Some species of parasitic bees invade a colony and kill the queen, and then they lay their own eggs in the host's cells and force the host workers to raise the young parasitic bees.

Vulture bees (family Meliponidae) are a special type of stingless bees, first identified in 1982 by David Roubik, now at the Smithsonian Tropical Research Institute. They seek out rotting carcasses and ingest their body fluids, which they process using saliva. They take this substance back to their nests, and, like nectar, it is passed to storer bees and transformed, and eventually it is fed to larvae. A recent report by Sidnei Mateus and Fernando Noll describes their observations of these neotropical stingless bees feeding on the living brood of social wasps in a recently abandoned wasps' nest.

Question 4: How are bees classified?

Answer: All the species on earth are classified in a taxonomic system that organizes the evolutionary relationships among all the species. Taxonomy is hierarchical, with the highest categories as the most inclusive and the lower categories as the most restricted. The names of the categories are domain, kingdom, phylum, class, order, family, genus, and species. (Students of biology make a silly memory device to remember the order of these categories, using the first letters of the names; co-author Elizabeth Evans remembers them using "kangaroos play chess on fuzzy green squares.") The three domains of life are the Bacteria, the Archaea, and the Eukaryota.

All animals, including bees, are members of the Eukaryota domain. Bees are members of the kingdom Animalia, the phylum Arthropoda, the class Insecta, and the order Hymenoptera (from the Greek *hymen,* for membrane, and *pteron,* for wing). This order includes over one hundred thousand diverse species of bees, wasps, ants, and sawflies that have been identified and described. Characteristic of most members of this order is a "wasp waist" or narrow area between the thorax (middle body-part) and the abdomen (end body-part). They also all have two pairs of wings, multi-segmented antennae that are usually longer than the head, and chewing mouthparts. The females typically have a sting on the ovipositor (egg-laying organ), and a few species have a piercing ovipositor. Hymenoptera undergo complete metamorphosis (see sidebar on metamorphosis in chapter 2), and the males usually develop from unfertilized eggs. Many of the species in this order are social and live in colonies that can be quite large.

After four years of work by hundreds of scientists, the sequencing of the 236-million-base genome of the European honey bee *Apis mellifera* was completed in 2006. This is the fifth insect that has been sequenced to date, and already over ten thousand genes that influence social behavior and physiology have been identified. This new information has been hierarchically organized into a system called ProtoBee to facilitate further study by scientists around the world (see http://www.protobee.cs.huji.ac.il/index.php?global=protobee|no|4|444|lifetime|1|2|2).

Evolutionary relationships among the thousands of bee species that have been classified will undoubtedly continue to change as more information is analyzed, as is happening in the taxonomy of other animals for which the genome has already been mapped.

Question 5: What is the earliest evidence of the existence of bees?

Answer: In 2006, a bee fossilized in amber was purchased by entomologist and amber aficionado George Poinar of Oregon State University. The amber came from an area in Myanmar (northern Burma), and it is estimated to be one hundred million years old. The bee encased in the ancient petrified sap is thus the earliest known bee pollinator. It belongs to the genus *Melittosphex,* and is described as from "an extinct lineage of pollen-collecting Apoidea, sister to the modern bees," although it has some transitional features. While some of the first plants were larger than their current versions, the early flowers were quite small when this small bee lived, and it was just the right size to pollinate them. In fact, its hairs actually still hold a few grains of pollen.

Genotyping by Charles Whitfield and colleagues at the University of Illinois at Urbana-Champaign determined that the European honey bee came to Europe from Africa in at least two population expansions, which explains why honey bees in eastern and western Europe are genetically different, although their habitats are adjacent. European bees were introduced to the New World by settlers in the seventeenth century, and they have been genetically modified recently by the arrival of African or so-called killer bees, *Apis scutellata x mellifera,* with which they mate. This influx began in Brazil in 1957 (see chapter 9, question 5: Do killer bees really exist?).

Question 6: Where in the world are bees found?

Answer: There are now bees on every continent except Antarctica, but that was not always true. The temperature in Antarctica is so extreme that bees cannot survive, and the habitat can't sustain many flowering plants to serve as their food supply. In fact there are only two flowering plants on the southernmost continent, Antarctic pearlwort (*Colobanthus quitensis*) and Antarctic hair grass (*Deschampsia antarctica*); the flowers of both plants largely remain closed and self-pollinate.

There were no honey bees in the New World prior to human European colonization, although the climate was hospitable to them. European honey bees were introduced by colonists into North America soon after they arrived. In New England, the English immigrant William Blackstone reportedly was unsuccessful in his efforts to grow apple trees until honey bees were brought over in 1623 to provide pollination. Colonists in

Australia and New Zealand also imported honey bees from Europe to pollinate their crops and to provide honey and wax.

Question 7: Do all bees make honey?

Answer: No, in fact most bees do not make honey. Of the approximately twenty-five thousand known species of bees, only seven species with forty-four subspecies are recognized as honey bees that produce and store honey. There are some other related bees that also produce and store small amounts of honey, but only members of the genus *Apis* are considered true honey bees.

In Europe and America, the most common type of honey bee managed by beekeepers is the Western, or European, bee (*Apis mellifera*), which has many subspecies, or regional varieties, including the European dark bee (*Apis mellifera mellifera*), the Italian bee (*Apis mellifera ligustica*), the Carniolan honey bee (*Apis mellifera carnica*), and the African bee (*Apis mellifera scutellata*). There are other species of tropical honey bees in Asia, including the red dwarf honey bee (*Apis florea*), the Eastern hive bee (Apis cerana), and the common giant honey bee (*Apis dorsata*). Subspecies differ in color, anatomy, and behavior, depending on the habitat to which they have adapted.

Question 8: Are there different types of bees within one hive of honey bees?

Answer: A honey bee colony is a large social group made up almost totally of females, traditionally described as being like a factory within a fortress, efficiently guarded and run by sterile females in the service of their queen. Recent developments in molecular research have made it possible to rapidly and easily obtain a genetic profile of the members of a colony, and scientists using these new techniques indicate that the traditional concepts may be oversimplified. For example, Madeleine Beekman and Ben Oldroyd at the University of Sydney studied one particular subspecies of *A. mellifera,* and for that population they estimated that from 10 to 50 percent of workers from other colonies were successful in sneaking past the guards of another colony and entering the hive, with the intention of parasitizing the colony's resources and possibly even laying eggs that could be fed and cared for unwittingly by the hive bees that attend the queen's eggs.

So the answer to this question is more complex than was true in the past—there are probably more types of bees within one hive than anyone would have imagined, and we will discuss the new data as we describe life in the colony. But the basics remain the same: a honey bee colony typically consists of as many as fifty to seventy-five thousand bees, and all or most of them are the female offspring of one queen. There are a few hundred drones and one queen, unless the queen is not functioning normally and a transition to a new queen is in progress (see chapter 8, question 2: What is swarming?).

Question 9: What is the role of the workers?

Answer: Females do all the work of the hive, and their reproductive organs normally are not fully developed. This state is known as reproductive self-restraint, and it occurs because the cues the workers receive tell them that the queen is laying an adequate number of eggs. The cues come from the queen in the form of pheromones (chemical signals), including odors that mark the eggs as belonging to the queen. Even the larvae participate in this process, giving off chemical signals, specifically, aliphatic acids, that influence the suppression of the worker's ovaries, helping to keep the workers focused on their tasks and not distracted by instincts to reproduce. That being said, Madeleine Beekman and Ben Oldroyd found that approximately 1 percent of the workers in the European honey bee colonies that they studied had active ovaries and were able to lay eggs (see chapter 5, question 5: How does the queen control the hive?).

Adult bees do not increase in size as they grow older, but their role in the hive changes as they age, and this process creates the division of labor in the colony. Their age-related transitions to different roles occur not because of hereditary differences, but

Fig. 4.   All worker honey bees are females. Just as the queen is specialized for egg laying, worker bees are specialized for foraging. Their bodies are built to find and transport pollen to the hive. They have brushy hairs that pick up pollen as the bees visit flowers. Their forelegs have combs and brushes that push the pollen into clumps that fill the pollen baskets on their rear legs. *(Drawing by Julie L. Dlugos.)*

rather due to the degree to which groups of genes in the bee brain are activated. This activation results in behavioral change and is known as genomic plasticity. As a result of mapping the bee genome as isolated through bee brains, Charles Whitfield and his colleagues were able to predict the behavior of fifty-seven out of sixty bees by measuring the levels of activation of a large group of genes.

When a worker first emerges from her pupal case, she spends the first day or two letting her wings and exoskeleton harden.

Then she begins to work at tasks associated with the interior of the nest, including bringing food to the larvae in their cells and grooming the queen and the other workers. Until she is seven to ten days old, she consumes protein-rich pollen so that the hypopharyngeal glands in her head fully develop. These glands produce a fluid that she will feed to the larvae as her next task (see chapter 2, question 2: What do larvae eat?). As the bee ages, she moves on to keep the hive clean, make wax, and participate in building the honeycomb. When she is mature, which means about three weeks old, the typical worker shifts her attention to tasks that bring her in contact with the world outside the nest. These tasks include receiving nectar from foragers and placing it in storage cells, guarding the entrance to the nest, and scouting for food. The transition from working inside the nest to working outside the nest is a big change in the life of a worker bee. Flying back and forth to collect pollen and nectar is done

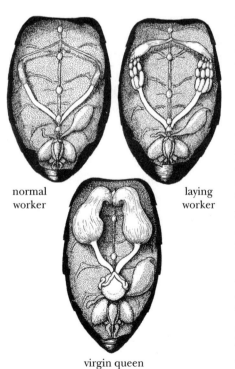

normal worker

laying worker

virgin queen

Fig. 5. Dissected views of the reproductive anatomy of worker bees and laying worker bees. All three images show the glands associated with the sting apparatus at the tip of the abdomen. The branched oviducts in the normal worker are undeveloped, but in the laying worker, they show evidence of egg formation. In the virgin queen, the round spermatheca is well developed and the ovaries are expanded, in readiness for egg laying. *(Used with permission from the International Bee Research Association; the original image was plate 17 in H. A. Dade,* Anatomy and Dissection of the Honey Bee *(London, U.K.: Bee Research Association, 1962))*

only by the most experienced bees in the colony during the last week or two of their lives (see chapter 2, question 4: How long do bees live?).

Several factors contribute to these behavioral changes, including hormones, lipid stores, neurochemicals, and environmental cues. Mark Drapeau and others have identified proteins, as a result of analysis of the bee genome, that play a role in reproductive maturation and stage-specific development. There are observable differences in gene expression in young nurse bees compared to mature foragers, and an increased expression of foraging genes was observed by Seth Ament and colleagues in the older bees. It can be difficult to tell if the increased activity of foraging genes in older bees causes foraging, or if changes in foraging gene activity are the result of foraging, but there is clearly a connection between the genetic activity and the behavior. Research by Charles Whitfield and his colleagues found that a brood pheromone that inhibits behavioral development is present in the crops (nectar storage pouches) of foragers at levels thirty times higher than it is in the crops of nurses. The foragers pass along the pheromone to the younger workers when they exchange food with them, and this inhibits the young bees' development by depressing the amount of juvenile hormone in their hemolymph (body fluid). When it is time for the workers to move on to tasks requiring more maturity, the amount of brood pheromone received by them is probably reduced and the foraging gene activity increases.

Andres Pierce, Lee Lewis, and Stan Schneider at the University of North Carolina have recently published observations that challenge some assumptions about the role of honey bee workers. They established that the colony's older workers play a very important role in the behavior within the nest before a swarm occurs. These scientists found that activity prior to and during swarming, including the activity of the queen herself, is regulated for the most part by mature foragers who use vibrations and movement to signal the queen and the other workers, guiding them through the various steps involved in swarming

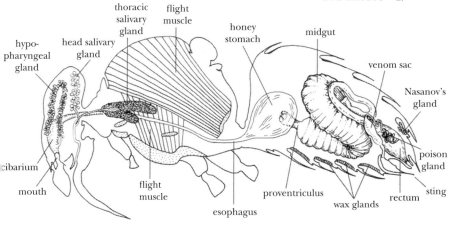

Fig. 6. A schematic diagram of the internal anatomy of a honey bee worker: note the position of the honey stomach, or crop, in the abdomen. (*From Thomas D. Seeley,* The Wisdom of the Hive: The Social Physiology of Honey Bee Colonies *(Cambridge, MA: Harvard University Press, 1995), 25. © 1995 by the President and Fellows of Harvard College. Adapted from original drawings by Barry Siler in* The Social Behavior of Bees, *by Charles D. Michener (Cambridge, MA: Belknap Press of Harvard University Press, 1974), 11. © 1974 by the President and Fellows of Harvard College.)*

and finding a new nest (see chapter 3, question 6: How do bees communicate? and question 8: What is piping behavior?).

As a footnote, recent research on ants by Fabian Ravary and Emmanuel Lecoutey in France found that successful foragers who were rewarded with prey on every trip foraged more and more, while foragers who had not been rewarded, and so were "unsuccessful," foraged less and moved on to other tasks. Whether this reward system in ants has any application to foraging bees is intriguing and remains to be investigated.

Question 10: What is the role of the drones?

Answer: Male bees are called drones, and only a small number of them exist in the typical colony at any one time. A drone develops from an unfertilized egg laid by the queen, so it can be said that he has no father, although he does have a grandfather on his mother's side. He is almost twice as large as his sisters, but he is not physically equipped to collect pollen or nectar, and he cannot help defend the hive because, being male, he has no sting (the sting is part of the female's egg-laying organ, the ovipositor).

The only role played by a drone occurs outside the nest. During a queen's first few days of life, she mates with several drones that find her while flying. Other than his role in this important process, he has no function in the colony and simply rests, grooms himself, and begs other bees for food. To help him locate a virgin queen with whom to mate, a drone's compound eyes are much larger than the same structures on female workers (so large that they touch on the top of his head). In addition he is equipped with antennae that are particularly sensitive to queen pheromone. If a drone has not successfully mated after a week or so of trying (see chapter 4, question 3: How do bees mate?), the workers will withhold food and he will weaken and die, or he will be driven out of the hive and killed because he is a drain on the group's reserves. The reality is that most drones

Fig. 7. A side view of a male, or drone, honey bee. Drones have large eyes and long antennae that they use for locating queens during mating flights. Their robust bodies are bulky compared to their sisters, the workers. If the colony is healthy, there are always many more workers than drones. (*Drawing by Julie L. Dlugos.*)

Fig. 8. In this photograph, the larger bee, marked by the arrow, is a male drone, surrounded by female worker bees. Note his body size, relative hairlessness, and his large eyes. *(Photo by Debra Cook-Balducci.)*

die before getting a chance to mate. Unless a colony is preparing to swarm or has recently swarmed, it is relatively rare to find drones in the nest.

Question 11: What is the role of the queen?

Answer: The queen is of great importance to the colony because she controls and regulates reproduction. When a new queen is needed, a larva from a worker egg is fed exclusively on royal jelly for her first four days of life (see chapter 4, question 7:

Fig. 9. A side view of a honey bee queen. Her large, bullet-shaped abdomen is filled with swollen ovaries and other specialized structures for egg laying. As females, queens can sting, but because they use their ovipositor both for stinging and for laying eggs, they don't often participate in nest defense. (*Drawing by Julie L. Dlugos.*)

What is royal jelly and how does it produce a queen?). The workers deposit a flood of royal jelly into the larval queen's cell, and she eats more or less constantly. This special diet triggers the queen's body to grow quite large and her reproductive system to fully develop, but her brain is smaller than the brain of a worker bee.

Once the adult queen has emerged from her cell, she goes on a series of mating flights over the course of a few days, and then for the rest of her life stays in the colony, laying eggs and regulating much of the activity of the hive by releasing chemical bouquets or pheromones (see chapter 5, question 5: How does the queen control the hive?). She is always surrounded by attendants who feed her, stroke her, carry away her waste, and guide her to empty brood combs where she lays an egg in each cell.

Honey bees are *haplodiploid*, which means that if they mate, the offspring from the fertilized egg will be female (*diploid*), but they are also capable of parthenogenic or unmated reproduction, which results in male offspring that have only half the usual number of chromosomes (*haploid*). The queen lays fertilized eggs in most cells, and they develop into female workers; but occasionally her attendants will take her to a larger cell,

The Honey Bee Colony as Superorganism

Many scientists whose work we discuss in this book study the behavior and characteristics of bees on the genetic level. Now that the genome of the honey bee has been thoroughly mapped, scientists have turned their attention to understanding the functions of individual genes and groups of genes in honey bees as well as in other social insects. According to Bert Hölldobler, an experimental behavioral biologist known for his research on ants and other social insects, "The more we understood about genetics, the more the focus was on the gene." And, indeed, the era of molecular studies has given scientists new tools for understanding the genetic basis of many different behaviors.

Classical evolutionary biologists say that genes are the units of natural selection, and that selection favors only behaviors that help the individual survive and leave more healthy offspring. Charles Darwin was puzzled about how altruistic traits could be propagated if individuals who show those qualities do not reproduce; he was particularly perplexed by the female workers in a honey bee colony that spend their sterile lives tending the queen's babies. How could traits they exhibit be passed on to subsequent generations? He eventually concluded that the target of selection can be the social group or family, rather than only the individual. This possibility was largely rejected by other scientists, given the popularity of the prevailing theories focusing on the gene alone as the unit of selection.

A new book by Pulitzer prize–winning authors Bert Hölldobler of Arizona State University and Edward O. Wilson of Harvard University focuses on the social group as an evolutionary unit. These scientists are animal biologists, not molecular biologists, and they specialize in the study of ants (myrmecology). Some of the ideas presented in their 2009 book, *The Superorganism,* are considered heretical by many evolutionary biologists, although the ideas have roots in the phenomenon

(continued)

The Honey Bee Colony as Superorganism, *continued*

Fig. 10. Although frequently called a "bee nest," these aerial, paper nests are constructed by the wasp called the bald-faced hornet, *Dolicho-vespula maculata*. These nests are annual; each spring, an overwintered, mated queen hornet initiates a new nest. Like bees and ants, wasps are considered to be "super-organisms." (*Drawing by John F. Cullum.*)

that puzzled Darwin. Hölldobler and Wilson suggest that selection occurs on multiple levels, including the level of the social group, and that the survival of one group of organisms can be favored over another because of genes that benefit the group, even if that success occurs at an individual's expense. From this perspective, the colony has characteristics of a species, and can serve as a model for illuminating the evolution of life forms as they became more complex.

In *The Superorganism*, the authors extend the focus of their 1990 book, *The Ants*, to include other social insects: wasps, bees, and termites as well as ants. They describe a cohesive colony of honey bees, for example, as a single animal, a "superorganism" or biological entity composed of units that are traditionally seen as individuals. Each individual worker bee functions like a cell, while the queen acts more like an organ system.

The Honey Bee Colony as Superorganism

She functions as the organism's genitals, while workers play the role of the supporting parts of her reproductive system.

The analogy can be expanded by considering the many different behavior patterns of individuals in the colony. Guard bees are the superorganism's immune system, and foragers are its eyes and ears. Thousands of little brains are connected in multiple ways, communicating with great intensity and complexity using a variety of taps, strokes, dances, noises, and chemicals. An elaborate division of labor is maintained, foraging and territorial strategies are conceived and executed, and castes (in the form of major behavioral changes that occur as young adult bees become foragers) are controlled completely by pheromones, climate, the availability of food and water, and the fecundity of the queen, rather than by precise genetic changes.

Many scientists are exploring concepts that underlie the nature of the superorganism. One particular area of interest is to understand how a division of labor is possible among thousands of female workers who are sisters with essentially the same genetic makeup. We know that physical and behavioral changes can occur in an individual without changes to the structure or expression of its genes. The changes may result, for example, from the impact of climate or other environmental conditions on the organism. Many predators and foragers evolve behaviors that reflect the opportunities and limitations imposed by the availability of prey, nectar, or other resources. In the case of social behavior, an individual's behavior may be influenced by its gene-filled environment, meaning the organisms with which it interacts. For example, generosity or aggression is, by necessity, expressed in a social context: the phenotype and genotype of the social partners that are objects of the behavior may influence the evolution of the behavior of the subject. In a similar manner, but on a broader scale, the superorganism responds and evolves in response to its environment.

(continued)

The Honey Bee Colony as Superorganism, *continued*

The superorganism concept is of great interest to students of systems theory, an interdisciplinary field dedicated to the study of complexity in nature, science, and society. A car is an example of a relatively small technological system, and a nuclear power plant is a system that is much larger and obviously much more complex. A system can be analyzed in terms of its reliability, and predictions can be made as to how it will function over a specific period of time. This theoretical approach to understanding complexity has implications for the risk management of any system or organized group, including accident prevention, insurance premiums, and pension contributions. Even the best system, when under repeated stress, will experience fatigue, resulting in cumulative damage and eventual system failure. For biologists applying system theory to the understanding of social evolution, system failure parallels what can happen to social insect superorganisms under stress.

Gro Amdam, a University of Arizona biologist who uses the honey bee as a model organism to study how social behavior and longevity are regulated, has applied the superorganism analogy to understanding disease. The honey bee colony has to defend itself against pathogens and parasitic bees that deplete its resources, and these intruders survive as long as they are not recognized. Once an entity is recognized as foreign to the system, it is killed; this parallels the immune system attacking cells that are intruders in the body. When an organism recognizes cancer cells as non-self, the body's immune system tries to destroy them and eliminate the disease.

The superorganism idea is controversial and fascinating, and even those who disagree with its premise cannot help but be intrigued with this way of thinking about bees and complex social systems. This latest book by B. Hölldobler and E. O. Wilson is a useful resource for those interested in the evolution and maintenance of social behaviors.

which will stimulate her to lay an unfertilized egg that will develop into a male.

Although in most species workers do not reproduce, the reproductive habits of Cape honey bee workers (*Apis mellifera capensis*), a southern *South African* subspecies of the *Western honey bee*, have been recently studied with surprising results. Unmated Cape bee workers are uniquely able to lay *diploid* (female) eggs by means of *parthenogenisis*, whereas unmated females of other honey bee species are only able to lay *haploid* (male) eggs. Females of this species have been found by Michael Lattorff and colleagues at Martin Luther University in Germany to have the capacity to develop into "pseudoqueens," which he defines as workers with queen-like physiology and behavior. Using genetic analysis, the Australian researcher Lyndon Jordan and his colleagues found that twenty-three out of thirty-nine new queens produced by seven colonies of Cape honey bees that they studied were offspring of workers rather than of the colony's queen, and only eight of the new queens were from eggs laid by workers from the same colony. The others were offspring of workers from other colonies that had entered and parasitized the colony's queen cells, and three of the daughters of the resident queen were clones (produced asexually). These discoveries suggest the complexities that are being unraveled by researchers now that DNA analysis is available and the honey bee genome has been sequenced. The main browser for the honey bee genome is available at BeeBase (http://racerx00.tamu.edu/bee _resources.html).

Question 12: Why are bees important?

Answer: Bees have been valued since ancient times for their honey and for their productivity. In cultures where bees are common, they symbolize work, creative activity, cooperation, orderliness, and diligence; and to be "busy as a bee" is a universal compliment. Honey and beeswax production is valued at approximately 285 million dollars annually in the United States alone.

Honey bees play a critical role in agriculture by pollinating crops, and in the United States alone, it is estimated that approximately twenty-four billion dollars worth of crops require pollination, most of them grown on large monoculture farms (farms that grow only one crop). A huge industry has developed that provides managed honey bee colonies for commercial crop pollination. Trucks containing up to a thousand or more hives transport bees to wherever a crop needs pollination; the bees are released for the required period of time and then recollected and moved elsewhere. The cost of renting bees for commercial pollination in the United States was estimated recently at around ten billion dollars (see chapter 6, question 5: How do farmers make sure there are enough bees to pollinate their crops?).

TWO

Bee Bodies

Question 1: How does a honey bee develop from an egg to an adult?

Answer: The honey bee queen lays an egg in a small chamber or cell in an area of the colony called the brood nest. A helpless, grub-like larva emerges from each egg after a few days, and its only function is to eat. Unlike a butterfly caterpillar that must forage for food, the bee larva never strays from its cell and nurse bees (young adult worker bees that perform this task at a particular stage of their life) constantly deliver food, sometimes flooding the cell with food. It has been estimated that more than one hundred thousand visits are made to a single honey bee during its egg and larval stages, during which time the larva can increase in size one-thousand-fold (see this chapter, question 2: What do larvae eat?) Because it doesn't leave its cell, the larva's bodily wastes are stored inside its body to protect the food in the cell from fecal contamination.

All honey bees outgrow their "skin" and molt about every twenty-four hours during the first few days of larval life (see chapter 2, question 10: Do bees have bones?). Their skin is actually an external skeleton or *exoskeleton,* and when the *ecdysis* or molting occurs, the skin splits at the head and slips off the rear end of the larva's body in a process that normally takes less than thirty minutes. Underneath is a new skin that is softer and looser at first, filling up as the larva grows until it is stretched tightly

Metamorphosis

Bees undergo complete metamorphosis, which involves a significant change in both their internal and external form (morphology). The word is from the Greek word *metamorphoun*, meaning "to transform," a compound of the words *meta* (after or beyond) and *morphe* (form). The familiar transformation from a tadpole into a frog is another example of complete metamorphosis.

Complete metamorphosis in an insect involves four basic stages:

- It starts with an egg containing an embryo.
- A bee larva hatches from the egg, basically a simple grub-like eating machine that outgrows and sheds its outer skin five times. This process is called molting, and the skin is actually its skeleton, called an exoskeleton. Each time the old exoskeleton is shed, a new, looser version is revealed underneath that fills up as the larva eats. A complicated series of hormonal fluctuations accompanies each molt.
- The fully grown larva's last molt reveals the pupal stage, during which the exoskeleton totally encloses the insect and it stops eating. Within the pupa, the bodily structures reorganize, unnecessary body parts are discarded, and the insect is totally transformed.
- A fully grown adult insect emerges from the pupa.

About 12 percent of insects, including crickets and grasshoppers, go through *incomplete* metamorphosis that skips the pupal stage. The adult female lays her eggs and the eggs hatch into nymphs that look like small adults but usually don't have wings. They molt several times as they grow until they reach their adult size, by which time they have usually grown wings. In contrast to metamorphosis, a cockroach and a human are examples of a continuously developing animal that begins as a small version of its adult self and just grows larger, the only structural change being the development of its reproductive organs and, in insects, fully developed wings.

again, signaling that it is time for another molt. Each stage before the molt is called a numbered instar, and after the fourth instar has grown to its maximum size, several things happen. Prompted by hormones (internal chemical changes) and phero-mones (external chemical signals), the larva stops eating and finally expels its feces, which are pushed down to the bottom of the cell. The nurse bees apply a wax cap that closes off the cell, and the larva spins a cocoon around itself using silk from a special gland in its head. Layers of silk may coat the brood cell walls, having accumulated from previous larval generations. The beeswax that makes up the combs can soften in warm weather, and the accumulated silk is thought to strengthen the cell and give extra protection to the pupae.

Soon after the cocoon is complete, the fifth molt occurs inside the cocoon and the pupa is revealed under the old exoskeleton. During the pupal stage, the larva metamorphoses into a fully grown adult bee. When the metamorphosis is complete, the bee ecloses, which means it sheds its cocoon, and then finally leaves the cell to begin its adult working life. Beekeepers sometimes describe the emergence of the adult bees from the pupal case as "hatching," a colloquial term for eclosing.

The length of each developmental stage differs slightly for each caste, although each caste spends about three days in the egg. The queen spends eight days as a larva, and after about four days in the pupal stage she ecloses. Female workers spend about eight to ten days as larvae and eight days as pupae. Drones spend about thirteen days as larvae and eight days as pupae.

Question 2: What do larvae eat?

Answer: Nursing worker bees bring the larvae a series of different foods as they develop in their cells. At each stage of growth, the larvae give off particular chemical signals (phero-mones) that tell the nurse bees what to feed them, resulting in qualitative and quantitative differences in the food given to lar-val queens, workers, and drones. The larvae that will develop into worker bees are first fed a *brood food,* also called *worker jelly,* which is produced by the hypopharyngeal gland in the head of a nurse bee. After about six days, the nurse bees begin feeding the worker larvae a combination of nectar and *bee bread,* which is a substance made from pre-digested protein-rich pollen. After three more days, the larvae enter the pupal stage, at which time they stop eating and live off their accumulated body fat, and over the next few days they metamorphose into adult bees.

The bee larvae that will develop into queens are fed exclusively on royal jelly for their first four days of life (see chapter 4, question 7: What is royal jelly and how does it produce a queen?). Drone larvae require the most food because they grow larger than either workers or queens, and the food mixture given to older drone larvae contains the most protein-rich pollen.

Other species of bees have a different way of feeding their young. (See chapter 1, question 3: How many species of bees exist?). In solitary species there are no nest mates to care for the young. Instead, the mother prepares a nest in soil or in another small space and she places a small pellet of pollen mixed with freshly collected nectar in the nest. She lays one egg directly on this larder, and when the larva emerges it eats this food independently, without any contact with adult bees. It subsequently pupates, metamorphoses, and emerges as a fully developed adult bee.

Question 3: What do bees eat?

Answer: Bees drink nectar from flowers, either directly or regurgitated and sipped from the mouth of another bee. When nectar is in short supply, they sip honey that has been collected in the hive. Bees also require water, and Per Kryger and colleagues from the University of Aarhus in Denmark report that the task of foraging for water is carried out by approximately 1 percent of honey bees that are the same age as nectar and pollen foragers. In the desert, some bees forage for water as far as a mile (about two kilometers) from their colony, carrying it back home in a storage pouch, called a crop, located in their abdomen.

Adult bees have a tube-like *proboscis* with a tongue that sits inside it, and unlike butterflies and moths that use their proboscis like a straw to suck up watery nectar, almost all bees lap or lick up nectar that is more concentrated and sticky. This difference in the preferred consistency of the nectar is probably one of the many factors that determine which flowers will be a nectar source for each animal, allowing them to share the resources of the habitat.

A bee's tongue is encircled by rings of hairy cartilage at regular intervals, and the tip of the tongue is a small spoon-shaped lobe that is smooth on the underside and covered with branched spines along the edges and top. As the bee laps at fluids using muscles that control the tongue, a muscular sucking pump in the bee's head draws the liquid up through the proboscis. The food travels from the proboscis along a very narrow passageway through the bee's brain to the digestive system in the abdomen.

In a remarkable experiment in published in 2003, evolutionary biologist Brendan Borrell surgically removed the tongues from over seventy orchid bees (*Euglossa imperialis*), a species that has a proboscis that is longer than its body. These bees typically feed from flowers with thinner nectar than most bees prefer, and Borrell's experiments showed that these bees could efficiently drink the thin nectar (a 35 percent sugar solution) without a tongue, strongly suggesting that sucking plays a big role in their normal eating. Bees with tongues to lap the nectar in the usual bee-like manner did better with thicker solutions (around 55 percent sugar).

Question 4: How long do bees live?

Answer: As for all living things, bees' longevity is influenced by their environment as well as their genes. Under normal environmental conditions, a queen honey bee lives an average of one to two years, sometimes even longer. Unlike workers, who usually never develop a functional reproductive system, the honey bee queen remains reproductively viable throughout her

Epigenetics

Evolution has commonly been thought to occur primarily as a result of natural selection of the organism with the fittest set of genes, but natural selection does not act on genes—it acts on phenotypes. This is a critical concept. The term *phenotype* describes either the total physical appearance or constitution of an organism or a specific trait such as size, behavior, or coloring. Research has discovered that phenotypes can be influenced by environmental cues such as temperature and diet as well as by hormones, neurochemicals, and the composition and location of the DNA within the nucleus of a cell. The capacity of a phenotype to change—its plasticity—plays an important role in evolution. *Epigenetics* is the field of biology that studies changes that occur above and beyond the gene, without a mutation having occurred to modify the DNA sequence.

In the wild, the larvae of the Pipevine Swallowtail butterfly *Battus philenor* are predominantly black when they develop where the climate is cool and mostly red at temperatures greater than 86 degrees Fahrenheit (30 degrees Celsius). The red larvae are more tolerant of higher temperatures and their growth rate doesn't slow down in the extreme heat, while the black larvae don't do as well when it gets really hot. This is an example of how genetically identical organisms reared under different environmental conditions can display diversity in physical characteristics and behavior. Other butterfly phenotypes that have adapted to experimental environmental manipulation, usually involving heat-shocking or cold-shocking the larvae or pupae, are its flight patterns (*Pararge aegeria*), egg size (*Bicyclus anynana*), pupae color (Nymphalidae, Papilionidae, and Pieridae), and body size (*Hypolimnas bolina*). The shells of certain snails, *Nucella lamellose,* also show evidence of phenotypic plasticity. They grow thicker as a defense when they are exposed to the effluent discharge from the predatory native red rock crab *Cancer productus.* When they are experi-

Epigenetics

mentally exposed to the effluent from a relatively unfamiliar species of crab, they do not adapt defensively in response to its presence, although perhaps they would eventually adapt if that predator became a constant in their environment.

In the honey bee, anatomical, physiological, and behavioral characteristics differ among the behavioral castes, all of whom are females with the same genetic makeup. The behavior of a typical female honey bee changes from being totally occupied with nursing tasks in the hive when she is young to foraging outside of the hive in the last few weeks of her life. It has been shown that bees have some plasticity as to the age at which they begin foraging, and we know that this behavioral change is coordinated with the nectar flow and conditions within the colony—this is epigenetic regulation of aging. For example, if there is a shortage of food, more foragers are needed and somewhat younger than usual bees will begin foraging. And reversion from foraging back to brood care was reported in 1996 by Zhi-Yong (now Zachary) Huang and Gene Robinson under experimental conditions they created in colonies populated only with older, forager-aged bees.

In 2003, in order to study the differences in gene expression in the honey bee brain without having to consider age as a factor, Charles Whitfield, Amy Cziko, and Gene Robinson created colonies that were composed entirely of young bees. In the experimental colonies, some bees began foraging as much as two weeks earlier than usual, and as the colony aged, the lack of young bees caused some individuals to continue working as nurses even though they normally would have aged into becoming foragers. The researchers were able to study the brain gene expression profiles of bees of the same age in the role of young nurses, young, precocious foragers, older foragers, and older, overage nurses. These four groups were compared to nurses and foragers from typical colonies,

(continued)

for a total of six groups composed of sixty bees. The result was "a strong association between brain gene expression and behavior" demonstrating "a molecular 'signature' in the individual bee brain that is robustly associated with behavior." The researchers recognized that future experiments were needed to determine which genes are responding to environmental cues and which genes cause the behavioral changes.

Research to identify which genes are involved in responding to environmental cues and causing phenotypical differences in behavior became possible when the *Apis mellifera* gene-sequencing project was completed in 2006. Investigating the differences in genetic expression between queens and workers, Angel Barchuk, Robert Kucharski, Ryszard Maleszka, and their colleagues at the Australian National University, using data from the gene-sequencing project, found 240 genes that had different levels of expression in developing queens as compared to workers. A group from the same lab went a step further and demonstrated that the social behavior of honey bees is encoded in two groups of these genes: nine genes comprising what they labeled as the Major Royal Jelly Protein family and five genes encoding the yellow protein family. Their findings suggest that the typical royal jelly diet fed to future queen bees appears to modify the female bee larva's DNA in these groups of genes, resulting in different patterns of genetic expression in the queen than in a worker-caste female.

Subsequent results from the same lab explored DNA methylation as a key component in a network of factors controlling the reproductive division of labor among honey bees. *Methylation* is a type of chemical modification of DNA that has the effect of reducing or increasing the activity of a gene without changing its basic structure. In the latest experiment, one group of honey bee larvae were injected with a substance designed to inhibit DNA methylation, and another group of larvae were injected with a control substance. The researchers found that silencing the DNA methylation resulted in a pattern of gene expression that mimicked the pattern of larvae that were fed royal jelly, and, indeed, 72 percent of the larvae in that group developed into bees that were queen-like with fully developed ovaries. Seventy-seven percent of bees injected with the control substance became workers. The way in which these different patterns of gene expression influence the development of the bee's brains is a subject for further study.

Other researchers have described "tool kit" proteins that produce substances, called *morphogens,* that have the capacity to influence the development of cells. Morphogens are active at particular locations, and they activate DNA that tells the genes at a particular location on the wing of a butterfly, for example, to make an eyespot (part of its characteristic pattern). Research is also ongoing on the role of hormones in mediating the functioning of the genes. The ebb and flow of hormones regulate stages of development, and research is focused on the role of hormones when the organism is subjected to extreme environmental influences. An example of this occurs in humans when an adult female is extremely overweight or underweight. Under those circumstances, it is not unusual for her reproductive system to be dysfunctional and for ovulation to cease. Other factors known to affect phenotypic plasticity are the degree of looseness with which the DNA thread is wrapped around its protein spool and the variability of the location of the DNA within the nucleus of the cell.

Now that we are beginning to understand some of the subtleties of how genes function, the evolutionary relationships among phenotype, genotype, and the environment are being slowly revealed.

life. This is quite unusual since most organisms have decreased longevity the more they reproduce, and the mechanisms behind the queen's longevity are being investigated.

Drones have a very limited but important role in the colony and a very limited life. Their only function is to mate with a virgin queen. Otherwise they have no function in the colony. If the drone is successful in mating, he will normally die soon afterward (see chapter 4, question 3: How do bees mate?). If he has not successfully mated after a week or so of trying, the workers will withhold food or he will be driven out of the hive and killed because he is a drain on the group's reserves.

The hive bee caste consists of young worker bees and performs a variety of tasks inside the nest for from nine to forty days, usually ranging from eighteen to twenty-eight days. As they mature, they become members of the forager bee caste, the group that ventures outside the nest to engage in the riskier activities of guarding the nest and collecting nectar, pollen, and water. Foragers live for one or two weeks if they emerge from their pupal stage in the warm weather and if they begin foraging when nectar production is high. If they are *diutinus,* or "winter bees," having emerged in the fall and reached the foraging stage in the cold weather, they can live six months or more. During the winter the colony is cold and inactive, and the winter bees live a quiet life inside the nest, eating only small amounts of honey, taking up their roles as foragers when flowers begin to bloom in the spring.

Stig Omholt and Gro Amdam at the Agricultural University of Norway studied the role of a yolk protein called *vitellogenin* that they hypothesize plays a role as a lifespan-promoting protein. The age-based division of labor among worker bees, where the risky task of foraging is only taken on by older workers with depleted nutrient stores, seems to have evolved as a mechanism to conserve the resources of the colony. Healthy winter bees show few signs of aging during the long winter period of inactivity, although their protein stores become gradually reduced until pollen and nectar become available again in the spring. Then they start nursing and foraging and their life ends in a few weeks following the usual warm weather cycle. The researchers calculated that if winter bees were prevented from becoming active, they could live more than two years based on the gradual rate of reduction of their protein supplies during the winter.

Mapping the honey bee genome has made it possible to observe that genetic activity is quite different in young nurse bees compared to mature foragers. Although the normal aging process usually triggers this behavioral development from nurse to forager, a shortage of food can prematurely induce this transition because there is an increased need for foragers to search for food for the colony. Experimental manipulation has been able to reverse the hive bee to forager bee transition, so that a nutrient-deprived older forager can be rejuvenated into a nutrient-enriched healthier bee. With enough food and time to build up their protein reserves, the biological pathways leading to the resumption of vitellogenin synthesis were apparently activated, and old bees became capable of functioning like younger bees. Natural selection seems to have endowed honey bees with some degree of behavioral flexibility within the age-based division of labor in order to ensure optimal allocation of resources for the colony. The implications of this research are profound, suggesting that honey bees may possess the capacity for epigenetic regulation of aging (see sidebar on epigenetics), although there is obviously a long way to go before these results can be generalized.

Question 5: Are bees intelligent?

Answer: A honey bee brain has fewer than one million neurons, while a human brain has around one hundred *billion* neurons. Bees are capable of a wide range of behaviors, although they have a brain the size of a peppercorn and a nervous system that is simpler than many other animals. At one time, scientists believed that insects were not very interesting to study with regard to their intelligence, assuming that their behaviors were stereotypical and fixed—more like robots than living things. We now know that many insect behaviors are dependent on

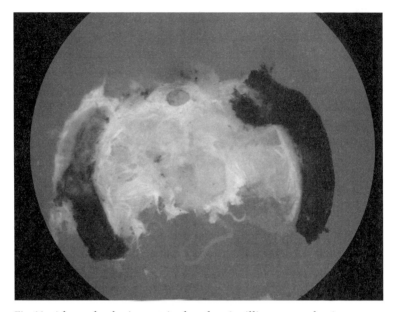

Fig. 11. A honey bee brain contains less than 1 million neurons but is responsible for many complicated behaviors. The visual pigment of the compound eyes (*far right and left*) is seen on this image of a brain dissected from the exoskeleton of the head. (*Photo by Corey J. Flynn.*)

their capacity to assess local conditions and that they can adjust their behavior depending on their perceptions, much like vertebrates. This flexibility is especially true for bees and indicates a higher level of intelligence than other insects.

Bees see color and have well-developed olfactory (smell) and gustatory (taste) systems with a fondness for sweets. Included in their behavioral repertoire is an ability to learn the location and identity of their home as well as the spatial features of the local neighborhood, to identify nest mates with an awareness of social roles, and to learn about resource availability. Honey bees use a symbolic language and employ such basic concepts as sameness and difference. One indicator of intelligence is the ability to profit from learning experience, and bees' capacity to learn complex behaviors has been amply demonstrated. Because of

Bees' Learning Abilities

Bees are fast learners, something that has been demonstrated in many experiments that explore the range of their abilities. In a typical study building on the honey bee's sensitivity to color and scent, bees were taught to associate a smell with a specific color that led to a sugar reward inside a Y-shaped maze. If the smell was lemon, the bees learned that the sugar reward lay behind a blue door where the maze branched; if the smell was mango, they learned that the yellow door hid the sugar. In 2001, a team led by neurobiologist Martin Giurfa, then working at the Free University of Berlin, designed experiments to investigate the ability of bees to make decisions based on abstract concepts. Using a similar experimental design, honey bees were trained to associate colors and patterns with food rewards in a Y-shaped maze. These scientists found that when bees were shown a blue patch at the entrance to the tube, they learned to fly down the blue arm of the maze to find the sugar. Then when the entrance patch was changed to a pattern of bars, they chose the tube with the pattern of bars identical to the one at the entrance, promptly applying the concept of sameness to a novel situation.

Another study demonstrated that bees were able to learn behavior that would seem to be counter-intuitive. Foraging honey bees and bumblebees leave a scent mark on flowers with secretions from the tarsal glands at the end of their legs, and the scent usually repels other bees because it signals that the flower was recently visited and therefore is likely to be empty of nectar. Nehal Saleh and Lars Chittka of the University of London demonstrated that, contrary to what might be seen as instinctive behavior, bees can learn to identify scent marks as an attractant rather then a repellant if the marks are consistently associated with a reward.

Trophallaxis is the process by which a forager bee transfers regurgitated nectar to a recipient in the colony. The recipi-

(continued)

ent inserts her proboscis into the donor's mouth and drinks the liquid nectar and smells its floral scent. Mariana Gil and Rodrigo DeMarco demonstrated that even after only one of these relatively brief food exchanges, the recipients learned to associate the floral scent with food, so that when they were exposed by the investigators to the scent alone, they responded by extending the proboscis in anticipation of a meal. Similar experiments conducted by Walter Farina and colleagues at the University of Buenos Aires in Argentina demonstrated that scent information is transferred to long-term memory, which has implications for programming the recipient bees to seek the nectar source associated with the scent when they mature and become foragers.

A relatively new focus of research is on a type of social learning that can occur simply as a result of observing and imitating rewarding behavior. Until recently, most scientists thought that only vertebrates that have much bigger brains were capable of this type of learning, but a number of biologists have demonstrated that bees can learn this way, too. Ellouise Leadbeater and Lars Chittka observed that bumblebees are attracted to flowers where other bees are already foraging, apparently learning through observation which flowers are currently offering good nectar rewards. In their laboratory, bees were allowed to observe through a screen as a "demonstrator" bee chose to collect nectar at a source with a randomly selected color and location. Then seven alternative sources were placed in the same area, and when the observer bees where released, they clearly preferred the nectar source that was already occupied. A similar experiment with the same results was conducted by Bradley Worden and Daniel Papaj.

When visiting some flowers, carpenter bees *Xylocopa* spp. are considered nectar thieves, biting a hole in the base of a flower and drinking the nectar through the hole instead of from inside the flower, stealing the nectar without the payback of carrying pollen. Honey bees learn to make use of these

Bees' Learning Abilities

existing perforations to rob the nectar as well, not because the nectar obtained that way is particularly sweeter or greater in volume, as measured by Selim Dedej and Keith Delaplane, but simply because it offers a shortcut—a fast food alternative. Leadbeater and Chittka observed that bumblebees also rob nectar through existing holes, and then some of them adopt this behavior and bite into the base of flowers themselves. All of these learned behaviors give bees an advantage by minimizing their exposure to the dangers of being away from the colony because they can obtain nectar as quickly as possible and return to safety.

There is a fair amount of this type of research on honey bees because they are such rewarding subjects. As we learn more about their functioning on a molecular level, researchers are beginning to understand more about the functioning of the bee brain.

their highly social lives and sophisticated behaviors, bees are thought to be among the most intelligent insects.

The neural architecture of the honey bee brain is particularly intriguing. The small brain has many highly organized and sculpted regions that are easily distinguishable under a microscope. One of these brain regions, called the mushroom bodies (MBS) (formerly known as the corpora pedunculata), has attracted the attention of behavioral biologists and neurobiologists alike because of its unique size, shape, and connectivity. Mushroom bodies appear larger in animals that are highly social, and smaller in insects that live a solitary lifestyle. Neuroscientist Susan Fahrbach at Wake Forest University described the explosion of research interest in this part of the bee brain over the last decade. The discovery by biologist Ginger Withers and others, working at the University of Illinois in Urbana-Champaign, that honey bee brains exhibit neural plasticity during the life of an adult bee has initiated both behavioral and neurobiological studies with bees. Complex forms of learning and other cognitive processes, as well as brain structures, chemistry, and neurophysiology, have been explored in great detail by Randolf Menzel and his colleagues at the Free University of Berlin. These studies aim to connect the bee brain structures to their possible functions. The mushroom bodies appear to be involved with processing information acquired through both odor and vision, essential to the life of the bee.

Question 6: Does a bee have a heart?

Answer: Yes, bees have hearts, but they are quite different than the four-chambered hearts of mammals like humans. Bees, like all insects, have an open circulatory system without veins or arteries, so there are places in its body where the body fluid (hemolymph) washes directly around the tissues and organs. A pulsating, muscular tube along its back, called the dorsal vessel, pumps the hemolymph from the abdomen to the thorax and then to the head, squeezing the hemolymph into each section of the body. Additional pulsating organs, called simple hearts, or ostia, are located at other points in the body and boost the fluid's circulation. As the muscles relax, the fluid circulates back into the dorsal vessel, moving more or less quickly depending on the insect's activity level. Unlike blood, hemolymph does not carry oxygen, so this relatively inefficient system is adequate to distribute nutrients to the cells.

Question 7: Do bees bleed?

Answer: You may have heard it said that if you pull the leg off an insect it will bleed to death because it lacks a clotting component in its blood. This does not apply to adult bees, since their "blood," actually a whitish body fluid called hemolymph, does clot to prevent large amounts of fluid loss after an injury. Justin Schmidt wrote about doing research at the Carl Hayden

Bee Research Center in Tucson that involved "bleeding" bees to sample their body fluid, and he found that the fluid samples he extracted would clot in short order.

A bee's circulatory system does not move the body fluid under great pressure (see this chapter, question 6: Does a bee have a heart?), and this minimizes the loss of fluid until clotting has a chance to close an opening caused by an injury. Hemolymph also contains cells that, like human white blood cells, defend the body against infection and gather to close openings that penetrate the exoskeleton. Honey bee larvae do not appear to have a clotting system, but since they spend their entire time in a beeswax cell, injury or predation is unlikely with the exception of *Varroa* mites, which have become a threat over the past twenty years. These are external parasites that feed on the hemolymph of the developing larvae and create open wounds, making the larvae vulnerable to pathogens. If the larvae survive, there may be effects on their defenses or behavior that we do not yet understand (see chapter 10, question 3: What parasites and insects prey on bees?).

Question 8: How do bees breathe?

Answer: Bees breathe without lungs. Air enters through openings called spiracles on the sides of the bee body, and a network of tubes called trachea weave their way around organs and through tissues, allowing air to ooze throughout the bee's body. For larvae and inactive insects, this is how they breathe, taking in oxygen and expelling carbon dioxide through this simple system. But when a bee flies, it needs more oxygen and its flight muscles move more air through its body by expanding air sacs that are part of the respiratory system and drawing air in more forcefully. Then the spiracles contract and compress the air sacs, forcing the air deeper into the body so that more oxygen reaches the cells, and then the spiracles open and carbon dioxide is expelled.

Question 9: What do bees see?

Answer: Like many insects, bees have more than two eyes—they actually have five. The two largest are compound eyes that are set on either side of the head, each containing 4,500 individual hexagonal facets (*ommatidia*), which are light sensitive units that work together to produce an integrated visual image, although what they see is different from what we see. According to Lars Chittka and Nigel Raine at the University of London, the clarity of their vision is approximately one hundred times worse than normal human vision. This is because the number of ommatidia is relatively small compared to the 1.5 million photoreceptors in the human retina or the millions of light-sensitive elements in a digital camera.

Susanne Williams and Adrian Dyer at Monash University in Australia created an optical device that simulates the way multiple lenses create an image by using 4,500 parallel-mounted black drinking straws. Using this device, they concluded that in order to see fine details, bees would have to be very close to an object. Color plate D shows how, using their device, they illustrated what a flower might look like to a honey bee. Later work from the same lab applied this imaging system to the understanding of how bees navigate and recognize complex natural landmarks with incredible accuracy.

The bee's other three eyes are simple structures, called *ocelli,* that are located on the top of its head. These are light-detecting organs that do not produce visual images. They are common in some other insects; for example, some butterflies have ocelli on their genitalia. It is thought that they help the bee sense direction and low levels of light, and they may play a role in enabling bees to follow a streaking scout bee that flies overhead to lead a swarm to its new home (see chapter 8, question 4: How does the swarm locate its new home?). Bees are also able to see fast-moving objects much better than we can, and the ocelli may play a role in this facility. Recent experiments by Gerald Kastberger at the University of Graz in Austria explored how bees with occluded ocelli react to changes in the light environment during flight. He found that the ocelli seem to help control phototactic behavior in flight course control in honey bees.

Adrian Dyer has done a series of interesting experiments to explore the limits of bee vision. After much trial and error, he trained honey bees, *Apis mellifera,* to recognize an image of a human face by associating that face with a sugar reward, and they consistently flew to the familiar face when it was placed with other images that were unfamiliar. They even flew to that face when the sugar reward was removed. But when the face was rotated 180 degrees, they were significantly less able to identify it, raising interesting questions about their visual processing.

Bees are partially colorblind. Each ommatidum or facet in the eye contains nine light-sensitive cells that are receptive to different colors. They contain six green receptor cells, according to Motohiro Wakakuwa at Yokahama City University, which are responsible for detecting motion and seeing small targets. The other color receptors vary depending on their position in the eye, and there are now understood to be three types of ommatidia. So, for example, if the bee is looking down, certain receptors are sensitive to green light, but if she is looking up, they are sensitive to ultraviolet. The brain apparently compares complex sets of signals from different sensors to identify color.

Experiments have demonstrated that honey bees can see a wide range of colors, but the spectrum visible to them is shifted into the ultraviolet range, so they can tell the difference between yellow, blue, green, and ultraviolet but cannot distinguish between red and black. They can also see a color, known as "bee's purple," that is a mixture of yellow and ultraviolet, and they can see patterns of polarized light that help them navigate (see also chapter 3, question 13: How do bees sense and use polarized light?). Rudiger Wehner and Gary Bernard demonstrated that most photoreceptors in a bee's eye are "twisted like a corkscrew," and they found that the amount of the twist corrects for the potentially false perception of colors as a result of polarized glare from reflecting surfaces on plants.

The interior of a bee colony is quite dark and yet the bees inside do all sorts of detailed work, so clearly bees can "see" in the dark; touch and scent play a large part in organizing their activities inside the colony. Because they are red/black colorblind, meaning they cannot distinguish between these two colors, observation hives and bee labs are commonly lit with red lights so that researchers can watch them while the bees carry on in what seems like normal darkness to them.

Question 10: Do bees have bones?

Answer: Instead of a bony internal skeleton, adult bees, like all insects, have a firm scaffolding, called an *exoskeleton,* that encases the outside of their body. The external covering hardens after the bee emerges from the pupa, and it protects the bee from drying out, gives the bee support, and allows for movement. All of the bee's muscles are attached to this exoskeleton, which is jointed but very solid and durable. It is also coated with a thin layer of oily wax, secreted by the bee, which has an odor that is unique to her particular hive. Guard bees use these odors to compare to sensory information from the colony to determine if a bee trying to enter the colony is a nest mate or an intruder.

Question 11: How do bees' wings work?

Answer: Bees, like most insects, have four wings, two on each side. Normally, there are two larger forewings positioned in the front of the bee's body and two smaller hind wings toward the rear. When a bee is not flying, the hind wings are folded back under the forewings and it may look as if the bee has only two wings. Other insects (flies, in particular) actually only have two wings, so the four-wing design is not essential for flight.

With rare exceptions, such as the male desert bee *Perdita portalis,* which has atrophied flight muscles and does not fly, bees are hardy fliers with large flight muscles and excellent maneuverability. Insect wings don't simply flap up and down, but rather the tips of the wings move in an oval pattern and turn over during each stroke. When the wing travels downward, the topside faces up, and then the wing rotates on an axis before the

Fig. 12. The two sets of bee wings are marked by a series of veins that vary in their dimensions by species. The forewing is longer and toward the front of the bee's body, while the hind wing is shorter and toward the abdomen. (*Drawing by Julie L. Dlugos.*)

upstroke, creating a large amount of lift. The two types of wings can be hooked together during liftoff for flight when higher power is required.

Question 12: What are the antennae used for?

Answer: A bee has two antennae, sometimes called feelers, and the name "feelers" describes what these appendages do for bees. Each antenna is a major source of environmental information, with sensors that detect odors and function as giant external noses. Other antennal sensors are mechanosensors that detect wind direction and pressure waves, including vibrations, and they help the bees stay attuned to their body position in the environment. Using a microscope to examine the honey bee antenna reveals the complexity of these sensors. See also chapter 3, question 1: Can a bee hear?

Question 13: How do bees hold onto slippery surfaces?

Answer: Like all insects, honey bees have three pairs of segmented legs. There are antennae cleaners on the forelegs (See chapter 3, question 4: How do bees keep themselves clean?) and hairy "pollen baskets" on the hind legs. At the end of each leg are small hooks, called tarsal claws, that allow the bee to hold onto some slippery surfaces. The center part of the foot, between the tarsal claws, contains a structure called the *arolium*. Accord-

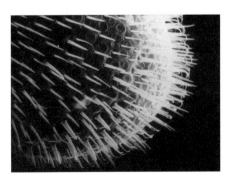

Fig. 13. A scanning electron micrograph of a worker honey bee antenna, showing the many hair-like sensors that detect odors and pressure waves. *(Image by Armand Whitehead.)*

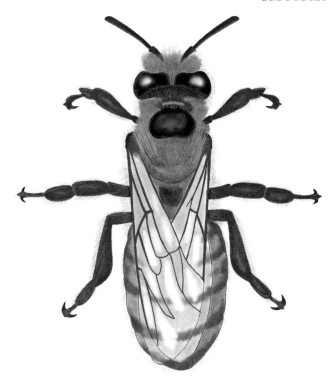

Fig. 14. The top view of a worker honey bee body. All six bee legs are attached to the middle body section, the thorax. The hair on the thorax is worn away as the bee ages due to repeated inspections of cells in the beeswax combs. *(Drawing by George C. West.)*

ing to famed honey bee anatomist H. A. Dade, this pad-like area essentially acts like a small suction cup to help the bee adhere to a slick surface (such as glass, plastic, or vegetation) when the claws cannot grip the substrate. There is also a tarsal gland that is covered with a thin, sac-like fold that forms a reservoir, and it probably fills and unfolds when the bee walks, also helping it to grip smooth or slippery surfaces.

THREE

Bee Behavior

Question 1: Can a bee hear?

Answer: Honey bees do not have ears, but they are able to sense certain frequencies, picking up the vibrations from the air or from the physical structure of the hive. Leg sensors called *subgenual* organs are fluid-filled channels that are attuned to these structural vibrations and conduct movements of the leg to sensory cells in the bee's brain. In addition to the sensors in their legs, bees have hearing organs on their antennae that are sensitive to certain frequencies.

The *flagellum* is the end segment (the third) of the bee antennae, and it is a highly sensitive detector of air particle movement, especially of low intensity stimulation in the 250 to 300 Hz range. Vibrations in this range are generated by the air flow from wing and abdominal movements produced by a dancer doing the waggle dance just millimeters away from the forager with whom she is communicating (see this chapter, question 7: What is the waggle dance?). The cues from these vibrations are transmitted to the brain by the Johnston's organ, located in the pedicel, or second section of the antennae. Only the antennae of older foragers are sensitive to these particular frequencies, and this restricts dance communication about food resources to the forager bees. Other areas of the antennae sense vibrations at frequencies used in piping behavior, a method used to communicate within the hive and to control swarming (see this chapter, question 8: What is piping behavior?).

Question 2: Is taste important to a bee?

Answer: It may seem strange at first, but bees have relatively little need to taste their food. A project completed in 2006 that examined the honey bee genome found that bees have only ten receptor genes for the sense of taste, compared to fruit flies with sixty-eight or mosquitoes that have seventy-six. Honey bee larvae spend their entire larval lives completely sequestered in a cell, eating whatever the nurse bees bring to them, and even in solitary species the larvae emerge onto a pile of food that was put in place when their mother laid their egg. So neither type of bee larvae needs to taste or select its food. Younger adult honey bees are in a similar situation when they are "hive" bees, always in the nest, eating whatever has been brought into the hive by older foragers. Venturing out of the hive to forage is the riskiest phase of life for a bee.

Bees have a mutually beneficial relationship with plants, in comparison with agricultural pests that need to be sensitive to the toxins some plants use to repel them. Fragrant flowering plants attract the forager bees and reward them with nectar for providing pollination—a simple transaction. The bees are in a hurry to return to the safety of the hive, so they will collect nectar from any flowers that are in bloom nearby and they do not have a big investment in finding the best-tasting nectar. Evolutionary ecologist James Burns reviewed a study of bumblebees and found that if they foraged for nectar hastily and indiscriminately, even if they occasionally visited flowers containing no nectar, they tended to collect more nectar than bees that spent time evaluating whether or not a flower contained nectar before they visited it.

In contrast to the behavior of bumblebees that visit multiple species of flowers, honey bees, in the course of a single foraging trip, tend to seek out flowers of the same species, a behavior known as flower constancy. Understanding why some bees are flower constant and others have more variable diet choices is the subject of a published review by an international group of scientists, Lars Chittka, James Thomson, and Nick Waser. They found that flower constancy is explained differently by scientists studying plant ecology (who ask, How does this animal behavior benefit the plant?), those interested in floral evolution (who ask, How are floral traits selected by bee behavior?), or those who study bee foraging (who ask, How do bees learn?). Psychophysicists L. Chittka and Johannes Spaethe observed the behavior of foraging bees and described the complex elements involved in their choice of floral targets, which included the role of speed, the making of productive choices, the presence of distractions and dangers, the intensity of the light, and the complexity of obtaining nectar from a particular flower. Notice that taste is not described as an important element.

Theodora Petanidou of the University of the Aegean in Greece analyzed the sugars in seventy-three plant species in the Mediterranean area and found that they contained various combinations of sucrose, glucose, and fructose, with traces of ten other minor sugars. Bees show a preference for high-sucrose nectars, while butterflies, in contrast, tend to prefer nectar with a lower sucrose content, effectively minimizing competition for the resources in the habitat. Jacobus Biesmeijer and colleagues from Leeds University in the United Kingdom did similar work in Costa Rica observing two species of stingless *Melipona* bees, both of which also showed a preference for sucrose over glucose and fructose. They reported that *M. beecheii*, a yellowish bee, preferred to forage in sunny patches which by their nature produce higher sugar concentrations, while *M. fasciata*, which has a dark brown body, foraged in shady spots but sought out nectar that was highly concentrated. These species divided the resources based on safety and potential camouflage rather than on taste.

Question 3: How do hungry bees share food?

Answer: A hungry bee approaches a sister bee and places her proboscis into the sister's mouth. This triggers a response in the sister: if she has food in her crop, she will regurgitate some of the food so that the hungry bee can ingest it from inside her mouth. This mouth-to-mouth transfer of food is known as *trophallaxis* (see color plate E). Both bees stroke each other's antennae while engaging in this behavior, and research has demonstrated that the antennae are an important part of this process because the bees are exchanging both olfactory and gustatory information. According to author and bee enthusiast Sue Hubbell, researcher John Free, while working at the Rothamsted Institute in England, found that the antennae were essential in making bees feed one another, and those bees that had lost their antennae were fed less often. In one experiment she describes, bees tried to feed freshly severed heads with intact antennae, and they even tried to feed cotton balls in which antennae-like wires had been inserted.

Recipient bees can learn the odor of a food provided by a donor bee in a single trial. Mariana Gil and Rodrigo De Marco at the University of Buenos Aires in Argentina found that honey bees' recall is better when the odor of the donated food is more concentrated. These observations support the idea that bees are exceptionally proficient at learning cues that will be useful for them when they need to locate valuable food sources in the future.

Question 4: How do bees keep themselves clean?

Answer: Bees are very hygienic animals—they don't like to be dirty or dusty. Keeping their bodies clean is a good way to keep debris out of the colony, reducing the chance that bee nurseries will develop infections and decreasing the likelihood that food supplies will be contaminated. Moreover, if a honey bee's eyes or antennae are soiled, their sensors might not function correctly, and that would be detrimental to the entire colony unit because it might put them at risk.

Honey bees have body parts specifically designed to help them stay clean, including a variety of bristles on their limbs that they use to clean body parts they can reach themselves, such as the mouth, proboscis, and antennae. The most notable cleaning structure is called the antenna cleaner, a peculiar-looking notch

Fig. 15. A specialized leg structure called the antenna cleaner allows honey bees to keep their antenna free of debris. Bees pull their antenna through these C-shaped notches on their forelegs before departing on flights. (*Drawing by John F. Cullum.*)

on the foreleg of a honey bee that is designed to slip over the antenna and remove any dust, pollen, or debris. After foraging and before flying home, honey bees will clean their eyes with their forelegs, and they will then pull their antenna through this special notch to clean up. These behaviors are stereotyped and always happen as a bee decides to head back to the hive.

When James Thomson at the University of Toronto observed certain bumblebees, *Bombus bifarius,* he found that their self-grooming as they flew between flowers sometimes significantly reduced the amount of pollen they dispersed to other flowers. Lawrence Harder at the University of Calgary reported that the amount of in-flight grooming by *Bombus* spp. depended on the pollen-dispensing mechanism of the plant; if the bee was disturbed by the accumulation of pollen on its body, the bee was more likely to self-groom. Marielle Rademaker and colleagues in the Netherlands tried to measure how much pollen was actually transferred from flower to flower by using dye to replace the pollen, and they estimated that *Bombus terrestris* removes 44 percent of the pollen grains when it visits a fresh *Echium vulgare* flower, and approximately half of the removed pollen adheres to the bee. Only a small fraction of the pollen grains on the bee were deposited on the stigma of the next flower, and a larger fraction was lost through grooming and through deposition on other parts of the flower (see sidebar: What is pollination?).

Grooming is an ordinary activity that is common among bees, but a very specialized honey bee *Apis mellifera* that seemed to be "compulsive" about social grooming was described by Darryl Moore at East Tennessee State University and colleagues. They named the bee Red 93, and she groomed other bees with her mandibles 84 percent of the time she was under observation. She never developed into a forager at the normal age of approximately twenty-one days, and even when she was thirty-one days old she was still dedicated to grooming other bees; the authors report that she is the most highly specialized bee groomer on record. Only twice among the 315 observed acts of social grooming was her grooming invited by the recipient bee. On all the other occasions, Red 93 simply approached a nest mate and directly began cleaning one or more of her body parts for a brief period, usually less than a minute. She then would immediately initiate contact with a nearby bee and commence grooming it. Uncharacteristically specialized behavior in bees has been observed by others on a few occasions, and it raises many intriguing questions about how the mechanisms that regulate behavior can go awry.

Under normal circumstances, honey bees perform a grooming invitation dance to solicit grooming from a nest mate. They stand in one spot and rapidly vibrate their body from side to side, sometimes stopping briefly to self-groom. Benjamin Land and Thomas Seeley at Cornell University determined that bees performing this dance are far more likely to be groomed by a nest mate than bees that do not solicit grooming in this way. When the researchers puffed chalk dust onto the base of the wings of bees in their experiments, they found that those bees danced more than bees that only received puffs of air, suggesting that the particles may trigger a need to be cleaned and hence the dance. In other observations of honey bees conducted by Janko Bozic and Tine Valentincic at the University of Ljubljana in Slovenia, they noted that the bees being groomed held their wings at right angles to the body, and that groomer bees tended to clean parts of the body that the receiving bee could not reach herself, usually removing dust and pollen from the base of the wings and realigning body hairs.

Bees also engage in grooming behavior to rid themselves of mites. U.S. Department of Agriculture biologists Robert Danka and Jose Villa provoked five hundred honey bees to groom themselves by placing a tracheal mite on each individual bee using an eyelash mounted on a small stick. Some of the bees were genetically mite-resistant and some were from a susceptible strain. They watched each bee for seven minutes and observed that resistant bees groomed themselves more often than susceptible bees, and they groomed themselves more on the side of the body where the mite had been placed, suggesting an awareness of the intruder. Grooming was similarly found by Frederic Ruttner and H. Hanel to be an effective defense used by some honey bees against *Varroa* mites.

Question 5: Why do bees buzz?

Answer: Sometimes buzzing is just the sound of bees at work, and sometimes bees use buzzing and other noises to guide their nest mates (see this chapter, question 8: What is piping behavior?). The sounds are not vocalizations, nor are they defensively directed against predators. The bees vibrate their bodies and their wing muscles in different ways and the vibrations resonate through the hive (see this chapter, question 6: How do bees communicate?). They cool the hive and help dehydrate the honey by beating their wings, which makes a buzzing sound. Bees buzz less in hot weather because they beat their wings more slowly to reduce the risk of overheating themselves. Queen honey bees announce a threat to the nest by making quacking noises. They are also said to toot. Quacking and tooting noises are together described as queen piping: these noises are produced by rapid contractions of the bee's thoracic muscles and occur without wing movement. The sounds are transmitted by being reflected from the beeswax substrate.

Question 6: How do bees communicate?

Answer: A honey bee's survival depends on social recognition and communication with other bees in the colony, so it is natural that bees are expert communicators, using sight, touch, movement, chemical signals, and, although they do not have ears, a sensitivity to certain vibrations that they feel with their legs and antennae. They communicate about finding food, avoiding or ejecting predators, and about conditions within the hive. There may be a surplus or a shortage of food, overcrowding, a need to start building more comb, or a queen who has stopped laying eggs—each of these situations requires a group response that has to be orchestrated.

Nobel prize–winning research by Karl von Frisch revealed that bees do different "dances" in order to tell the other bees where they have located a good nectar source. Their specific movements indicate the direction and distance of the nectar source from the hive (see this chapter, question 7: What is the waggle dance?). Sound and vibrational signals exchanged by honey bees during the performance of waggle dances have been studied extensively and recorded. The dances have been analyzed using a microphone and a laser vibrometer (an instrument that measures and analyzes vibrations without the need for physical contact with the subject), and a great deal has been learned about this direct, symbolic, movement-related form of transferring information. Kristen Pastor and Thomas Seeley studied bees that follow waggle dancers and make brief piping signals, apparently trying to beg for nectar from the dancers. They found that none of the dancers gave nectar to the bees that piped them, but the piping did seem to stimulate some of the waggle dancers to stop dancing (see this chapter, question 8: What is piping behavior?).

One of the most impressive feats of communication occurs when a queen and thousands of workers have swarmed, leaving an overcrowded colony and searching for a new nest site (see chapter 8, question 2: What is swarming?). The swarm flies out of the colony and waits as a group, perhaps all clustered on a tree branch, while hundreds of scouts fly out to search for suitable space. The scouts return and, over time, agreement is reached on which of the sites they have explored is most suitable, and the swarm takes off for its new home.

Thomas Seeley from Cornell University and Kirk Visscher from the University of California at Riverside tried to learn how this incredibly complex choice is made by closely monitoring four swarms as they engaged in this group decision-making process. They rejected the hypothesis that a consensus is somehow reached and suggested that the bees may sense a quorum when the scouts become aware that a particular site is being visited by a sufficiently large number of scout bees, perhaps as small a group as ten or fifteen bees. Using the dance, these bees somehow lead the group to approve of that site, and the decision is then communicated to the bees in the swarm by workers piping (see this chapter, question 8: What is piping behavior?). The result of this "quorum sensing" is that the swarm lifts off and moves to the new location.

Worker bees also communicate with vibration signals that are different from the waggle dance. In this multipurpose form of communication, one bee grabs another worker or the queen and rapidly vibrates her own body for a second or two while in contact with the other bee. Kristen Pastor and Thomas Seeley speculate that vibrating another bee seems to energize the recipient and causes her to alter her behavior. Prior to a swarm, workers vibrate the queen hundreds of times an hour, and she responds by reducing her food intake, slowing egg laying, and becoming more active. Then workers begin piping "at a fevered pitch," which stimulates bees to warm up their flight muscles and results in the swarm taking flight (liftoff) out of the nest. When the queen has left the nest with the swarm, the piping in the nest ceases. Andres Pierce and colleagues observed that workers rarely or never vibrated the queen inside the swarm, but piping continued in the swarm to stimulate the bees to fly again once a new nest site was selected.

In another form of communication, honey bees do a tremble dance to signal other bees not to fly off to search for more nectar because there is too much already arriving at the hive. Bees receiving tremble signals move to collect food from returning foragers instead. Corinna Thom and her colleagues were able to demonstrate that short piping signals made by workers had some relationship to the tremble dance, but this aspect of the nectar-foraging communication system is not completely clear because the behaviors were not universal among the dancers; virtually all of the piping signals were made by tremble dancers, but less than half of the dancers piped. The researchers speculated that the brief piping seemed to have some relationship to recruitment by the tremble dancers, but clearly more observations are needed.

A sense of smell is very important for bees as part of the colony's communication system so that order can be maintained in the hive through the use of pheromones or fragrant chemicals that play a role in virtually all of the hive's activities (see chapter 5, question 5: How does the queen control the hive?). When the honey bee genome was mapped, 170 odorant receptors attested to the honey bee's remarkable sense of smell, compared to fruit flies with 62 odorant receptors and mosquitoes with 79. Experiments conducted by Charles Ribbands at the Rothamsted Experimental Station in England demonstrated that honey bees can perceive greatly diluted chemical scents and can distinguish between mixtures that contain only slightly different proportions of the same two scents.

Guard bees use sensory information about the colony odor to determine if a bee trying to enter the colony is a nest mate or an intruder. Margaret Couvillon and her colleagues at the University of Hawaii transferred wax comb from a "comb donor" hive to a "comb receiver" hive, and they found that guards in the comb receiver hive became more accepting of bees from the comb donor hive. This strongly suggests that the presence of the transferred wax comb changed the odor template of the colony and that the template is used by the guards to evaluate visitors, rather than the actual scent of each individual bee. In a fascinating and confusing finding based on the colonies they studied, Madeleine Beekman and Benjamin Oldroyd, working at the University of Sydney, Australia, maintain that, contrary to prevailing lore about the effective screening ability of the guard bees, it is not difficult for a worker to enter the nest of another colony. They estimate that 10 to 50 percent of non-nest-mate workers are allowed by the guards to obtain access to a colony, a finding they verified by genetic analysis of bees in the colonies they studied.

In a unique experiment that has yet to be replicated, Song-kun Su of the College of Animal Sciences in Hangzhou and colleagues from China, Australia, and Germany reported the successful creation of a mixed-species colony composed of the Asiatic bee *Apis cerana cerana* and the European bee *Apis mellifera ligustica*. Their work was not without problems, and several of their experimental colonies became unstable and many workers were killed, but they report successfully managing a colony with an *Apis cerana cerana* queen and a cohabiting mixed group of workers for more than fifty days. Despite the differences between the species, the two types of honey bees could communicate using the waggle dance. Obviously, there is a great deal more to learn about how bees communicate.

Question 7: What is the waggle dance?

Answer: The waggle dance is a form of communication that honey bees use to recruit nest mates to fly to various locations in their environment where there are good nectar sources. When a worker bee returns to the hive from a successful foraging trip, she can direct her sisters to the place where she found the food using the dance, which encodes information about its direction and its distance.

Many naturalists had observed bees waggling in their hives after foraging, but it wasn't until the research of Karl von Frisch that the meaning of the dance was decoded. He deciphered the recruiting function of the dance and experimentally determined how the bees translate their flight through the landscape into a flight plan for the bees in the hive. After years of research, we now know how the dance is organized.

The bees enter the hive and find their way to the brood areas of the comb, where they begin their dance. Recall that in European honey bees, the beeswax combs hang down in vertical sheets inside the colony. The brood area serves as the dance platform, and many unemployed forager bees wait in that area for flight instructions.

Two environmental cues, the position of the sun's azimuth (the angle of the sun against the horizon) and the force of gravity, are the bases for the information communicated in the dance. First, the bees note the direction of the sun's azimuth in relation to North, being the 0 degree position. Based on this system, the sun rises in the East at approximately 90 degrees and sets in the West at about 270 degrees. If you point toward the sun and then draw an imaginary line from the sun to the horizon, you can measure the direction of that point with a compass. The position of the sun's azimuth varies depending on the time of day, and the bees must somehow learn the rate at which the azimuth moves across the horizon. They take into account the season and latitude, both factors that influence the rate of change of the sun's position.

Inside the darkness of the hive, the bees use their memory of the sun's location and their sense of time to predict the real position of the azimuth. The bees appear to walk in circles as they dance, and they use the dance to point to their flight direction. The azimuth is represented by the direction "up" on the comb, and because the bees in flight measure the direction of their flight relative to the azimuth, they translate that direction on the comb. If they are foraging on flowers located in the same direction as the azimuth, they waggle in a line straight up. If they fly 45 degrees from the azimuth, then they produce their waggle on the comb in a similar angle. The waggle dance, then, is a systematic way for the bees to encode their three-dimensional

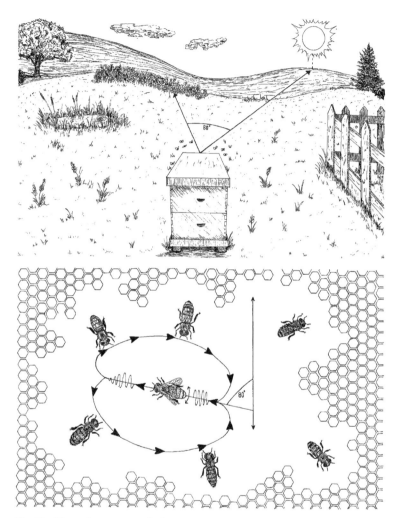

Fig. 16. Honey bees use symbolic movements to communicate the distance and the direction of profitable food sources to nest mates within the colony. The top panel shows the hive in the environment, and the bottom panel illustrates the bee dance at a moment in time. For details, see chapter 3, question 7. (*Drawing by John F. Cullum.*)

flight through the environment into a tidy, two-dimensional pattern on the comb. Figure 15 describes this directional signal in more detail.

The distance signal is encoded by the frequency of body vibration, or waggle. If the foraging site is located close to the hive, the waggle is brief; but if it is distant, the waggle is longer. The rate of the waggles is also affected by the quality of the food that the forager collected, so that if the sugar concentration is high, the dance is more vigorous and is repeated frequently; if the sugar content is low, the dance is not repeated. After a waggling run, the bees reset their signal by walking to the right, waggling again, and then walking to the left.

Dancing bees attract the attention of unemployed bees in the brood area, and these bees follow the waggle dances and make contact with the dancer's antennae as they move on the comb. The antennal contact allows the followers to detect the vibrational signals that come from the waggle. In addition, the dancer will stop between waggle runs and will feed small bits of nectar to her followers, which can then pick up floral odors from the dancer that serve as an additional recruitment signal.

Question 8: What is piping behavior?

Answer: Piping behavior describes a series of high-pitched sounds that reverberate through the colony. Karl von Frisch and others originally identified these noises as part of the language that the queen uses at particular times to assert her presence. Recent research has discovered that mature, forager-aged workers also pipe under particular circumstances, and a lot has been learned about this form of communication.

Picture the piping queen: she presses her thorax (the middle segment of her body) against the comb and vibrates her flight muscles without spreading her wings, producing short bursts of sound that are detected by other bees with sensors in their legs. The old queen (also called the mated queen) sometimes pipes before swarming, when the colony outgrows its hive and divides itself (see chapter 8, question 2: What is swarming?). After she has swarmed with a portion of the workers in search of a new nest site, one or more virgin queens normally are ready to emerge from their queen cells to supercede or replace her (see chapter 4, question 7: What is royal jelly and how does it produce a queen?). The first virgin queen to emerge produces piping sounds, and another queen that is still in her cell but is ready to emerge may respond with a deeper sound that has been characterized as quacking. The piping of the queen causes the workers in the colony to freeze in place until the piping stops, stopping their work of trying to release another queen by chewing away the wax and fibers capping her cell. This duet or dialog may continue for days at a time and may serve to suppress the emergence of an extra queen, which, if it occurred, would typically lead to a fight to the death.

Thomas Seeley and Jurgen Tautz described the piping behavior of mature workers as similar to queen piping, with the important distinction that the piping worker pipes other bees directly: the worker usually presses her body or head against the queen or a sister worker, pulls her wings tightly over her abdomen, and arches her abdomen downward. Then she vibrates her wing muscles and short, high-pitched bursts of sound are produced. An important function of this behavior is to cause the recipients to warm their flight muscles in preparation for "liftoff" prior to swarming, but workers may pipe the queen intensely for several days or weeks prior to the departure of the swarm, and the meaning of this behavior is not yet understood.

Andres Pierce and his colleagues were curious to see if piping continues once a swarm has left the nest, and they built an observation stand so that for the first time a swarm cluster hanging on a tree could be studied while the bees waited for scouts to guide them to their new location. What they found was fascinating. Workers seemed to pay little attention to the queen in the swarm until shortly before the time for liftoff approached. Then the pipers became quite excited, scrambling through the swarm cluster piping intensely and interacting with the queen at very high rates, and also piping workers at high levels, stimulating every bee to warm their flight muscles. When Seeley and Tautz experimentally removed piping bees from the outer layers of a swarm cluster and used an infrared camera to measure the temperature of the flight muscles of individual bees, they found that the bees did not warm up their flight muscles when the piping was absent. It is clear that piping behavior is a complex but very fundamental aspect of bee communication.

Question 9: Can bees tell time?

Answer: They don't wear wristwatches, but bees can certainly tell time. They are attuned to time in relation to the sun's position in the sky throughout the day. Bees can remember the time at which flowers have nectar and can use this information to guide their foraging choices. This timekeeping ability can be seen clearly in experiments conducted by Martin Lindauer in which bees were trained to feed from an artificial flower that provided sugar syrup at a particular time of day. The bees were able to learn to return to the feeder at that time, and while some scouts might look at the feeder at other times, a large majority of foragers returned when the time was right and the feeder was filled. Being time-sensitive is most likely an adaptation that enables bees to exploit food sources that are available during the hours of the day when nectar and pollen production is highest.

An awareness of the circadian clock (the day-night cycle) is involved in sensing the time as well as in navigation (see this chapter, question 12: How do bees navigate?), the division of labor, and the bees' dance language (see this chapter, question 7: What is the waggle dance?). The movements used to communicate about the location of nectar sources (the waggle dance) would be unintelligible to nest mates if a bee had a faulty sense of time.

Young adult bees, newly emerged from their pupal stage, typically engage in behaviors associated with tending the larvae in the brood combs, and the larvae are hungry around the clock with no particular sleep-wake cycle, not unlike human newborns. Like the babies, the nursing workers do not exhibit circadian rhythms, but they acquire them as they age and integrate into the light-dark cycle of the nest. The older adult workers, the foragers, have strong cycles, based on the daily clock, that are tuned to cycles of pollen and nectar production (see chapter 5, question 3: What do bees do all day?).

Guy Bloch and a team of researchers, using the honey bee genome sequence, identified a core group of "clock" genes that is responsible for circadian rhythms in honey bees. Interestingly, they found that the expression of the clock genes in the honey bee was more similar to the pattern in a mouse than in a fruit fly. The significance of this finding raises lots of new questions to be explored about the evolution of timekeeping behaviors. Why is clock gene expression in bees more similar to the expression in a mammal than in another insect? In what other ways are insects like mammals, and what does this tell us about the evolutionary conservation of molecules in various animals? Future research will undoubtedly explore questions like these.

The development of circadian rhythms in honey bee foragers is connected to the regulation of one of the clock genes, the period gene, well known for its role in circadian rhythms. Because the level of expression of this gene varies between nurses and foragers, we know that at least part of a bee's biological clock is associated with her social role in the environment of the nest. In recent research from the Hebrew University of Jerusalem by Yair Shemesh, Mira Cohen, and Guy Bloch, using a technique regularly used to study bee behavior and physiology, the researchers manipulated the social conditions in the nest by creating a colony of bees that were all the same age. In a process that is not well understood, some young bees adopt the behavior of the normally older foragers. Shemesh and coauthors found that the nurse bees could show sensitivity to activity cycles set by daylight when their social setting required it. They also found that the levels of gene expression in three other clock genes were lower or totally suppressed in nurses as compared to behaviorally cyclical foragers. This behavioral flexibility in the bees' circadian rhythms is associated with the organization of the internal clock on the molecular level.

Question 10: Do bees sleep?

Answer: The short answer is yes, indeed, bees do sleep, and they exhibit some of the same characteristics as humans when they are asleep: their muscles relax and they don't move around, their antennae become immobile in characteristic positions, they are less reactive to disturbances, and their body temperature drops. Walter Kaiser reported that, unlike mammals, bees sleep most deeply near the end of their period of sleep. A series of recent experiments and observations has been defining when and how bees sleep, and Barrett Klein has published his observations of sleep patterns in honey bees, reporting that their sleep patterns differ as they mature and as their tasks change from cell-cleaner to nurse to food-storer to forager. Younger bees sleep less often and less regularly, but the care for the brood is a round-the-clock job, so this is understandable. The circadian rhythmic sleep-wake cycle begins to be apparent in food-storers and becomes firmly established in foragers. Their active period takes place during the day, when they have access to nectar, so they sleep in a more predictable pattern, sleeping during the night for longer periods than the younger bees.

Stefan Sauer and colleagues arranged to deprive forager bees of sleep so that they could compare their sleep patterns with control bees that were allowed to maintain their normal schedule. Isolated bees were placed in a glass cylinder on a specially designed, motorized, tilting device with simulated daylight illumination. The tilting device produced a rolling movement of the cylinder, alternating with short pauses, which kept the bee awake during her normal twelve-hour sleep period. The exhausted bees compensated the following night with longer and deeper sleep, suggesting that, like in mammals, sleep is controlled by regulatory mechanisms. This conclusion is also suggested by the results of an experiment by Thomas Seeley and colleagues at Cornell University. They transplanted two colonies and trained the older bees to forage at particular times, and they found that the foragers shifted their sleep schedules so that they would be awake when resources were available.

Question 11: Do bees perceive magnetic fields?

Answer: There is some evidence that bees are sensitive to magnetic fields, but although it can be demonstrated that bees will react to changes in the local magnetic field, scientists can't explain how bees perceive it or the way they use it under normal circumstances.

Working at Princeton University, James Gould determined in 1978 that the abdomens of honey bees contain crystals of magnetite and that the bees' behavior could be altered based on artificially induced changes in the local magnetic field. Gould and colleague Joseph Kirschvink hypothesized that this substance could move within a cell and thereby convert or transfer directional information into the nervous system of the bee. Further studies conducted by learning expert M. E. Bitterman and colleagues demonstrated that the behavior of freely flying bees could be altered based on the magnetic field and that the application of magnets or magnetic wires to the bees could interfere with their behavior. There is evidence, then, that bees are sensitive to the magnetic field, or at least they are sensitive to alterations of the magnetic field; but, to date, no one has determined the degree to which this information is used. Most scientists believe that the magnetic field is used as a backup cue in the event that other, more salient cues are absent or provide ambiguous information to the bee.

Carolina Keim and others determined that there are iron-rich granules in bees' abdominal fat cells, but their research on the chemical properties and position of these granules led them to surmise that these substances are most likely *not* involved with magnetoreception, but probably are the result of the metabolism of iron from their pollen-rich diet.

Question 12: How do bees navigate?

Answer: The lives of the bees in a honey bee colony depend upon the ability of foragers to successfully fly as far as several kilometers to locate and collect nectar and pollen and then find their way back to the nest. They are considered a home-range species, defined as a navigating animal that can find its way over a relatively short distance, as compared to a migratory animal that travels quite far. Because this short-range navigational ability is so important to bees, they are "overengineered," as James Gould describes it, with an armament of several alternative methods based on various sensory cues that they use to find food. Axel Brockman and Gene Robinson of the University of Illinois at Urbana-Champaign have identified five different sensory systems that bees use to locate nectar sources and communicate their location to their nest mates, and they traced each sensory pathway to the location in the brain where it is processed (see also this chapter, question 7: What is the waggle dance?).

In simple terms, bees can see and smell the flowers when they get close enough, and if the sun is out, they can use a time-compensated sun compass, for example, keeping the sun to the left in the morning in order to fly south. They also are able to use distinctive landmarks as part of their orientation, a type of spatial memory that enables them to retain information about the location and orientation of particular details in their environment. Co-author Elizabeth Capaldi Evans and Fred Dyer studied the acquisition of visual spatial memory in honey bees and determined that bees rapidly learn the location of their hive on special orientation flights taken when they first depart from a hive in a new place. This large-scale spatial learning is similar to the learning that occurs when bees first explore new patches of food. The investigatory flights around the food were described as "turn back and look" flight by Miriam Lehrer, and were explored in more detail by Cynthia Wei and colleagues, who found that bees actively choose to spend less time on learning flights as they gain experience traveling to and from a foraging site. This finding is particularly interesting, as it indicates that bees can assess their own knowledge and can act to increase the contents of their memories. Certainly, this selective learning behavior indicates a higher level of cognitive ability than might be expected in an insect (see chapter 2, question 5: Are bees intelligent?).

Adrian Dyer and colleagues trained bees to recognize images of complex natural scenes and found that the bees were quite accurate in recognizing these landmarks and discriminating between a known scene and similar views that were introduced to confuse or distract them. Mandyam Srinivasan and colleagues in Canberra, Australia, trained bees to fly through short tunnels to collect a food reward and demonstrated with a series of experiments that their ability to monitor flight distances (their odometer) is visually driven, based on the amount of "image motion" that is experienced by their eyes as they travel along their route.

When the sun is not clearly visible, honey bees can use the pattern of polarized light in the sky as a navigational guide (see this chapter, question 13: How do bees sense and use polarized light?).

Question 13: How do bees sense and use polarized light?

Answer: The sun generates patterns of polarized light, especially in the ultraviolet range, and these patterns indicate the location of the sun when it is not directly visible on a cloudy day, or just before sunrise or just after sunset. Unlike the human eye that has receptors for only brightness and color, bees also have special receptors for ultraviolet and polarized light.

Remember that a honey bee has five eyes, three simple eyes and two compound eyes (see chapter 2, question 9: What do bees see?). Each of the compound eyes has 4,500 light sensors, called ommatidia, and there are three types of ommatidia, containing different sets of light-sensitive cells (spectral receptors), that are distributed over the retina in a pattern that is described by Motohiro Wakakuwa and colleagues as "rather random" and much more complicated than had been previously accepted. Rudiger Wehner and Stephan Strasser demonstrated that there is a group of about 150 specialized ommatidia in the uppermost dorsal area of the eye that has polarized ultraviolet receptors configured in such a way that they can translate the information from polarized light into "modulations of perceived brightness." This provides cues from which they can derive directional information in lieu of being able to see the sun. The researchers actually painted out different parts of bees' eyes and recorded their behavior, and these observations established that this group of specialized ommatidia is, indeed, the polarized light (POL) area of the eye.

The study of the homing abilities of bees has been a focal point of research because bees are excellent navigators. Foraging bees keep track of their distance and direction from the hive, and at any point on their journey they can turn and fly in a straight line, a beeline, back to the hive. Using the sun and the sun-linked patterns of polarization, the bees are attuned to their direction, and they use their ability to learn and remember the patterns in the landscape to guide their flight behavior. Some studies by Tom Collett and others by Rudiger Wehner indicate that bees' map-like spatial memories are arranged like overlapping beads on a string rather than like a typical geographic map. With their unique map and compass, these little insects can navigate up to ten miles away from their hive.

Question 14: Do bees ever get fooled by predators?

Answer: Unlike baiting a hook with a worm with the intention of trying to deceive a fish, mimicry is natural behavior of an animal trying to survive. Defensive mimicry may be more familiar, such as camouflage, where the subject tries to blend with the background, or Batesian mimicry, where a harmless species resembles a species that is toxic or harmful, duping predators into avoiding the safe prey because it appears to be harmful. In aggressive mimicry, a predator gives off signals that usually promise food or sex to their prey, and then they just sit back and wait for the prey to come to them. For example, the predator may look or smell enough like a female bee so that a male bee will be fooled into approaching.

In the Mojave Desert, a cluster of tiny, millimeter-long blister beetle larvae *Meloe franciscanus* give off a pheromone (a stimulating scent) that fools male solitary bees, *Hapropoda pal-lid,* into mistaking the larvae for a female bee ready to mate. When a male bee is attracted by their scent and attempts to mate with the ball of larvae, several hundred larvae attach themselves to the back of the unsuspecting bee as he struggles to get away. The larvae stay with the male, and when he actually mates with a real female bee, the larvae move onto the female; when she goes underground to lay an egg on her stockpile of nectar and pollen, they eat everything in sight, including the egg.

Some spiders are aggressive mimics that can lure bees into their webs. The golden orb weaver, also called the golden silk spider or banana spider, *Nephila clavipes,* attracts bees by spinning a golden-colored web in a brightly lit area; and while bees can associate other webs with danger, scientists speculate that the golden color of these webs mimics yellow nectar-bearing flowers and so attracts instead of warning the bees. *Argiope agentata* spiders attract bees by weaving patterns in the center of their webs that appear to mimic the nectar guides in the center of flowers. Small female crab-spiders (*Thomisus onustus*) mimic different flowers by adapting their entire body to the color of the flower and then making themselves inconspicuous on a petal until a bee comes to nectar, at which point they attack the bee.

In yet another variation of aggressive mimicry, some robber flies in the genus *Mallophora* closely resemble bumblebees, even down to hind legs that look like the pollen-carrying legs of the bees. When an unwitting bumblebee approaches the fly, it captures the bee and squeezes it tightly against its own body and then pierces a hole in the bee's body and feeds on its insides, leaving only the exoskeleton remaining. Aggressive mimicry takes many forms and is not unique to predators of bees; this mimicry subjects many insects, birds, and other animals to these types of seductive attacks.

FOUR

Bee Love

Question 1: How does a bee attract a mate?

Answer: Queen honey bees give off pheromones that attract males (drones) when they are ready to embark on their mating flights (see this chapter, question 3: How do bees mate?). Since the sole task of drones is to mate with virgin queen bees, it is unsurprising that drones have receptors on their antennae that are specially attuned to detect queen pheromone. When a virgin queen is ready to mate, she makes several flights to an area where drones from local colonies congregate and wait for a queen with whom they can mate. When the drones become aware of her presence, they compete to mate with her and some of the strongest and most agile succeed.

In solitary species, the males normally emerge before the females, and they may wait for a female to emerge at the nest site or near a flower and then mate with her there. Among bumblebees and some solitary species, the male is responsible for attracting a mate, and he marks a series of plant stems with pheromones that he secretes from glands on his mandibles (jaws). In some species, males are territorial and patrol and guard a certain route, marking it with pheromones. Sometimes other males are attracted as well, and when a receptive female is drawn to the territory, the male or the group of males attempts to mate with her, and in some cases a large mass of drones surrounding the female will fall to the ground in the midst of trying to mate.

Question 2: Do all bees mate?

Answer: Among female honey bees, it is almost always only the queen that mates. She mates multiple times shortly after she emerges from the pupal stage, storing up enough sperm to keep laying fertilized eggs for the rest of her life. The queen releases a pheromone that suppresses the development of the reproductive systems of the female worker bees. This chemical keeps the workers from becoming reproductively viable, and the queen's eggs and larvae reinforce her message with chemicals that they pass along to the attending workers, signaling that the queen is providing the colony with an adequate supply of new workers. If the queen is removed or if her pheromone level drops, worker eggs can develop, although, because workers are equipped with barbed stings, they cannot mate.

The only role of a drone is to mate with a virgin queen when she goes out on her brief mating flights. Drones do not mate with the queen of their own colony—that queen is the drone's mother. A virgin queen may mate with as many as twenty drones, but the rest of the drones will die without mating. If a drone has not successfully mated after a week or so, the workers will withhold food or he will be driven out of the hive and killed. The reality is that most drones die without ever mating (see chapter 1, question 10: What is the role of the drones?).

Question 3: How do bees mate?

Answer: A virgin honey bee queen mates early in her life, having sex "on the fly" with as many as twenty drones over a period of a few days, and then she never mates again. She produces eggs throughout her life in well-developed ovaries that fill up most of her abdomen, and she can produce hundreds of thousands of offspring in her lifetime from the sperm she stores in those few days.

A few days after the young honey bee queen has emerged from her pupal case, she flies to a so-called drone congregation area, where a large number of fertile males from nearby colonies are assembled, waiting to take advantage of their once-in-a-lifetime opportunity to pass on their genes to any virgin queen that comes along. The drones fly around at a height of twenty or thirty feet above the ground, and they locate a receptive queen by sensing her pheromones and by using all five of their eyes. If they are vigorous enough to catch up with a queen, they may get the opportunity to indulge in what has been described as an "acrobatic orgy."

This vivid description of honey bee mating comes from Mark Winston in his 1987 book, *The Biology of the Honey Bee.* "Mounting and copulating are rapid and spectacular . . . with the drones literally exploding their semen into the genital orifice of the queen." Once contact has been made, the mating generally lasts from one to five seconds. "Within a split second, the drone grasps the queen with all six legs and everts the endophallus into the queen's open sting chamber. At this point the drone becomes paralyzed and flips backward, and ejaculation results from the pressure of the drone's hemolymph as the abdomen contracts. The explosive and sometimes audible ejaculation ruptures the everted endophallus and propels the semen through the queen's sting chamber and into her oviduct" (page 207). The ejaculation separates the drone from the queen, and he dies shortly after mating.

Observers report that they can tell when a queen bee is mating nearby because of the large number of dying drones that drop to the ground, sometimes accompanied by a noise like popcorn popping. The drone's severed genitals may act as a temporary vaginal plug, designed to allow time for the drone's sperm to enter the queen's system, but the queen or a subsequent suitor can dislodge the plug, so no drone is guaranteed exclusivity. The queen receives an average of six million sperm from each male, but sperm die in large numbers as they make their way through the female's reproductive tract, and some may be ejected during the course of a subsequent mating. Stored sperm may even be digested in lieu of food in times of famine, so, typically, the queen will retain only about six million sperm from this mass mating to fertilize her eggs. In fact, this multiple mating (*polyandry*) assures genetic diversity that confers multiple benefits on the colony (see this chapter, question 4: Why does a queen mate with more than one drone?).

In some solitary species of the genera *Nomadopsis* and *Perdita,* the male may remain coupled with the female while she forages or flies back to the nest after mating, preventing other males from mating with her. *Centris adani* males deposit pheromones on the female during mating that repel other males. Male bees in these species also die shortly after mating, and the female begins searching for a place to build a nest. Some solitary females only mate shortly after they emerge from the pupal stage.

Question 4: Why does a queen mate with more than one drone?

Answer: Mating with more than one drone (up to twenty in the case of the honey bee queen) results in a genetically diverse colony, and scientists are discovering the benefits that result from the diversity, at least in the short term. The benefits of genetic diversity in the long-term are difficult to establish because, essentially, only the queen reproduces.

Using instrumental insemination (see this chapter, question 10: Can bees be artificially inseminated?) to create colonies that have been fathered by only one drone and comparing them to colonies where the queen was fertilized by mixed semen from several drones, Julia Jones and her colleagues at the University of Sydney found that the diverse groups were able to keep the temperature in their nests more stable than the genetically uniform colonies because bees from different lineages started fanning at slightly different temperatures, while bees in the homogenous colony all started fanning at the same time.

Other evidence of the adaptive value of genetic diversity was explored by Cornell University scientist Thomas Seeley in a study with Heather Mattila and in another with David Tarpy. Both studies compared genetically diverse colonies, where the queen had been instrumentally inseminated by sperm from ten or fifteen drones, to genetically uniform colonies, where the queen had been inseminated by sperm from only one drone. The genetically diverse colonies proved to be more resistant to bacteria, built honeycomb at a 30 percent faster rate than homogenous colonies, collected 39 percent more nectar and pollen, and after two months had five times the population of the single father colony. Swarms from diverse colonies also founded new colonies faster than swarms from genetically uniform colonies, another valuable attribute.

Paul Schmid-Hempel and Boris Baer in Zürich compared queen bumblebees that were instrumentally inseminated with sperm from the same drone with others who were inseminated with a mixture of sperm from four drones. The queens then founded colonies in a meadow near Basel, and their progress was tracked. The multi-father colonies were healthier, suffered from much less parasitism than the single-father colonies, and were twice as prolific, further confirmation of the benefits of genetic diversity.

Question 5: How many eggs does a honey bee queen lay in a day?

Answer: A honey bee queen can lay fifteen hundred to three thousand eggs on a good day, and she can lay as many as half a million eggs in her two- or three-year lifetime. Her eggs are only reared to adulthood if there are enough workers to feed and incubate them.

Question 6: How is the sex of a bee determined?

Answer: If a queen lays a fertilized egg, it will become a female worker or, potentially, a queen; if she lays an unfertilized egg, it will become a male. Each bee egg develops in one of a pair of small tubes (*ovarioles*) that make up the queen's ovaries, and once the egg is fully formed, it moves through the oviducts into a tubular passage (the *lumen*). A lifetime supply of sperm is stored by the queen in a little globular sac (the *spermatheca*) in her genital tract, and the queen controls the release of the sperm, enabling her to choose to lay an unfertilized egg or one that has been fertilized. When drones are needed in the colony, she will lay some unfertilized eggs. This peculiar system of reproduction is known as *haplodiploidy* because the drones are *haploid*, meaning they have half the normal chromosome content, and the queens are *diploid*—with a full set of chromosomes—like most animals.

But Soochin Cho and colleagues established that it is not quite that simple. In humans, sex is determined by the combination of sex-determining chromosomes derived from both parent's sets of genes (XX for females, XY for males). In the honey bee, specific combinations of different versions (alleles) of a sex-determining gene determine the sex of the offspring. If the bee has two different alleles, the sex-determining gene will be female; if it has only a single version of the gene, it will become a normal, fertile male. But if the queen has mated with a male who has a version of the sex-determining gene that is identical to hers, the fertilized eggs produced from his sperm that have two identical sex-determining genes will yield sterile male offspring, and these drones will be eaten by females in the colony since they cannot reproduce and therefore serve no purpose. Multiple matings reduce the proportion of sterile males that will be produced because not all mates will have a matching sex-determining gene. Jay Evans of the U.S. Department of Agriculture and colleagues have written a clear review of this sex-determining mechanism that was first identified by Martin Beye and others.

Question 7: What is royal jelly and how does it produce a queen?

Answer: Some people believe that the bitter-tasting, nontoxic royal jelly is a healthful component of the human diet, but scientific studies do not support that belief. But for a female honey bee, it makes the difference between developing into a queen or becoming an ordinary worker. A fertile queen and a sterile worker have the same genetic makeup (genotype), but they have very different traits (phenotype). The queen bee is large, mates and lays thousands of eggs, and can live for several years; a typical female worker bee has a reproductive system that never develops, is considerably smaller than the queen, and generally lives only several weeks. These differences occur, as the saying goes, because "you are what you eat."

Instead of being fed the usual brood food and bee bread, like a larva that is destined to become an ordinary worker (see chapter 2, question 2: What do larvae eat?), a larva that will become a queen is fed a substance, called royal jelly, that has a different chemical composition. Any female larva can become a queen if she is cared for properly by being fed royal jelly during the early stage of larval life. In the bee, the royal jelly causes a group of genes to be activated differently than they would be on a worker's diet, resulting in significant physical and behavioral differences (see sidebar on epigenetics in chapter 3). Hormones also function differently in the queen than in an ordinary female worker.

When the worker bees sense that the colony's resident queen is failing, they respond by creating some larger-than-usual cells, called queen cups, in the brood comb and encouraging her to lay eggs in them, so they can begin to rear a few new queens. A new queen must quickly supercede or replace the old queen if the colony is to survive. The worker bees produce royal jelly from a specialized gland (the *hypopharyngeal* gland) in the head, and they deposit a steady supply of it into the especially large cell where the queen larva is developing. Royal jelly is a thick, milky fluid with the consistency of plain yogurt, and it contains more protein and sugar than the food given to worker bee larvae. Royal jelly consists of approximately 12 percent sugar compared to about 4 percent in worker larvae food, and the queen larva is visited by nurse bees approximately 1,600 times, compared to 150 visits to a worker larva per day. These qualitative and quantitative differences produce dramatic results, and by the end of the larval stage, the queen is larger and heavier, she has a higher metabolic rate, and she has fifteen times the level of growth-stimulating juvenile hormone than that found in worker larvae at that stage.

Royal jelly also contains *vitellogenin,* an egg yolk precursor whose synthesis was investigated by Preeyada Koywiwattrakul, Graham Thompson, Sririporn Sitthipraneed, Benjamin Old-royd, and Ryzard Maleszka. The activity of the vitellogenin gene was found to be diminished or stimulated depending on the development of the ovaries. When groups of caged, queenless worker bees were treated with carbon dioxide (as is used as temporary anesthesia for artificial insemination of honey bee queens), they showed low levels of ovarian development as compared to controls that were not given the carbon dioxide treatment. The bees with inhibited ovaries had lower levels of expression of the vitellogenin gene. This finding may be of interest in understanding the regulation of sterility in worker bees. A queen's ovaries do not become completely activated until she mates, so when a virgin queen has been instrumentally inseminated, she is temporarily anesthetized with carbon dioxide, which stimulates her ovaries (see this chapter, question 10: Can bees be artificially inseminated?).

Question 8: How is the queen bee chosen?

Answer: There is no election process to become the new queen: she is not chosen, but presents the best traits among the queens that emerge. Once the old queen has swarmed (see chapter 8, question 2: What is swarming?), the first virgin queen that emerges from her cell is soon ready to take over as the reproductive focus of the colony. She begins signaling her presence with audible vibrations (see chapter 3, question 8: What is piping behavior?), which sometimes are enough to prevent any other virgin queens from emerging. This queen may also kill other queens in their cells before they can emerge. If another virgin queen manages to emerge, there may be a fight to the death between the queens. The departing queen is guided by a group of as many as ten or twenty thousand worker bees in a primary swarm. If more than one new queen emerges in the old colony and the first to emerge does not kill the others, there may be subsequent smaller "after" swarms, each led by a new queen.

Question 9: Can bees of one species mate with another species?

Answer: Honey bees cannot mate with other types of bees, like bumblebees or carpenter bees, but all of the breeds of *Apis mellifera,* the European honey bee, can interbreed. And bee-keepers can deliberately produce hybrids to improve disease

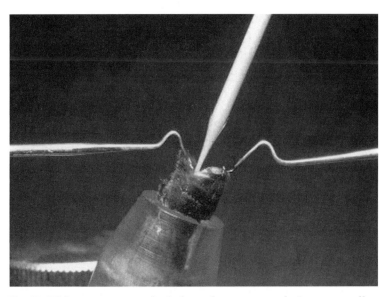

Fig. 17. With temporary anesthesia, honey bee queens can be instrumentally inseminated with drone semen using a laboratory apparatus. This close-up photo shows the process in detail. The queen's body is held in a small tube. While small hooks hold her abdomen open, a syringe deposits semen into her reproductive tract in a structure called the bursa (see chapter 4, question 10). *(Photo by Sue Cobey.)*

resistance and honey production and to create more prolific, gentle strains. Some of the advantages in the initial generations of deliberately created hybrids may be lost as subsequent generations crossbreed naturally. Some hybrids may
become unacceptably aggressive or may have developmental
defects.

Question 10: Can bees be artificially inseminated?

Answer: Artificial insemination of bees, known by beekeepers as *instrumental insemination,* was first demonstrated in 1927
after over one hundred years of failed attempts using all sorts
of imaginative techniques. Beekeepers are always trying to improve their stock by developing bees that are more disease resistant, better honey producers, and more docile. As the natural
survival of honey bees becomes more difficult (see chapter 10,
question 10: What is colony collapse disorder?), insemination is
being used for research and breeding experiments to try to un-
cover the causes of the decline. Researchers also use this technique to create colonies with certain characteristics that they
are interested in studying (see this chapter, question 4: Why
does a queen mate with more than one drone?).

In the 1940s it was discovered that multiple mating is normal
for queen bees, so when a queen is inseminated, semen is usually
collected from many drones and it is combined in a syringe. The
age of the virgin queens and drones at the time of insemination is important because they must be sexually mature. Queens
need to be from six to nine days old, and drones should be at
least sixteen days old. Collecting a drone's semen may be accomplished by holding him by the head and thorax and stimulating
the abdomen. It may be necessary to apply gentle pressure to the
tip of the abdomen in order for the endophallus (internal genital tract) to be everted so that the semen can be exposed and
collected. If this approach is not successful, the head and thorax
of the drone must be crushed and the endophallus forced out by
firmer pressure on the abdomen.

Fig. 18. A queen mating yard in Florida, with many small hives created to house new queens. Other nearby colonies rear drones to ensure that the virgin queens have ample mates. *(Photo by Gerry W. Hayes Jr.)*

The queen is placed in a holding tube and anesthetized with carbon dioxide, and the semen is injected into her reproductive tract. It may seem cruel that some drones are killed in the collection process, but since they die soon after mating naturally, their loss does not cause negative consequences to the colony (see this chapter, question 3: How do bees mate?).

FIVE

Bees in the Hive

Question 1: How many bees are in a colony?

Answer: Honey bee colonies can contain from ten to fifty thousand bees and sometimes more. Bumblebee colonies are much smaller, containing from about two hundred to four hundred bees. The population of a honey bee colony varies with the yearly cycle within the hive, so that it has the highest densities of adults, pupae, and larvae when nectar-bearing flowers are most available (see this chapter, question 10: Is there a yearly cycle in the hive?). The queen lays eggs whenever there is a net gain of food resources for the colony, and her egg production rate drops substantially as temperatures grow cooler and the day length shortens in the fall and new supplies of nectar become increasingly scarce. During the deepest cold of the winter, there is no brood rearing at all; but the colony begins to produce brood again in the very early spring, although there are no flowers blooming. Stored pollen is the primary source of protein during this early period, and the population increases so that there is a well-developed forager force in place for the flood of nectar when the spring flowers finally begin to blossom.

Question 2: How do bees construct their nest?

Answer: In their natural state, European honey bees nest in cavities like holes in trees and crevices within cliffs. Beekeepers tend managed colonies in wooden boxes, called hives, that

Honey Bee in Different Languages

Arabic	ب ينوه
Bulgarian	медоносна пчела
Catalan	*abella*
Chinese	蜂蜜蜂
Croatian	*pravo*
Czech	*včela medonosná*
Danish	*honing bi*
Dutch	*honings bij*
English	*honey bee*
Esperanto	*abelo*
Estonian	*mesilane*
Farsi	(ج.ش) زنبور عسل
Filipino	
Cebunao	*buyog, putyokan*
Hiligaynon	*ligob, putyokan, buyog*
Tagalog	*bubuyog, putakti*
Finnish	*mehiläinen*
French	*abeille de miel*
German	*Honigbiene*
Greek	*μέλισσα μελιού*
Hebrew	תרובד
Hindi	*Madhu makhi*
Hungarian	*méh, összejövetel*
Icelandic	*hunangsfluga*
Indonesian	*lebah madu*
Irish Gaelic	*beach*
Italian	*ape del miele*
Japanese	蜂蜜の蜂
Korean	꿀 꿀벌
Latvian	*bite*
Lithuanian	*bitė*
Malaysian	*lebah madu*
Norwegian	*bie*
Polish	*pszczoła*

(continued)

Honey Bee in Different Languages, *continued*

Portuguese	*abelha do mel*
Romanian	*albină*
Russian	пчела меда
Spanish	*abeja de la miel*
Slovak	*vcela*
Swahili	*nyuki*
Swedish	*honungbi*
Swiss German	*bienli, beili*
Turkish	*bal arısı*
Ukrainian	бджола
Vietnamese	*ong mật*
Welsh	*gwenynen*
Yiddish	*bin*

have removable frames of beeswax (see chapter 11, question 2: What does a beekeeper's hive look like?). When a swarm of bees moves into a new nesting space, their first task is to build out the sheets of wax combs that they use as a nesting substrate. As a part of the preparation for swarming, the bees will have consumed large quantities of nectar or honey, which primes their wax-producing glands (see chapter 6, question 9: How do bees make beeswax?). These bits of wax are called wax scales. They are chewed and sculpted into the familiar honeycomb pattern. As these workers continue to build, others begin to forage from the new nesting location in order to ensure that no bees, especially the wax-makers, go hungry while the new pantry is being built. Still other bees set up as guards to protect the new nest. The queen will generally walk around the comb, inspecting the cells for size and cleanliness before laying an individual egg in the bottom of each cell. Simultaneously, the workers will begin to fill nearby cells with pollen mixed with nectar (bee bread) in preparation for feeding the larvae that will soon emerge from the newly laid eggs. They deposit nectar around the periphery of the brood area, maintaining the brood in a central location close to the nest entrance as the colony grows, while the nectar is stored up and away from the entrance.

Question 3: What do bees do all day?

Answer: The saying "busy as a bee" undoubtedly arose from the impression one gets observing bees buzzing around a hive. Streams of bees zoom in and out, foraging and delivering nectar and pollen, and inside the hive they seem to be constantly in motion—eating, grooming, fanning, foraging, cleaning, building, and taking out the garbage. But researchers who have actually watched individual bees for days at a time, keeping careful track of their activities, tell a different story, and the results are a little disappointing: bees are really not all that busy.

In 1894, a scientist named C. F. Hodge watched a group of bees all day for several days. He reported that no bee worked more than three and a half hours a day. Typically, one bee might crawl into an empty cell and lay there for hours. In the 1950s, the behavioral physiologist Martin Lindauer followed up Hodge's work with a more comprehensive study, and he confirmed that a typical bee spent about two-thirds of her time doing no productive work at all.

European honey bees can't see well enough to forage at night, so this is when some honey bee foragers typically sleep. Barrett Klein working with Tom Seeley determined that honey bees shift their foraging schedules depending on when resources are available, and this dictates to some degree when they can sleep. Stefan Sauer and colleagues experimentally deprived foragers of sleep for a twelve-hour period in order to study their responses to the lack of sleep. Individual bees were placed into a glass cylinder with a light source equivalent to daylight and with free access to honey. The cylinder was secured to a motorized tilting device that produced one-second-long rolling movements, alternating with pauses of eleven seconds, effectively keeping the bees awake all night. The research team found that the exhausted bees compensated by sleeping more deeply the following night. Periods of time when their antennae were immobile were defined as sleep (also see chapter 3, question 10: Do bees sleep?).

Question 4: Do any bees forage at night?

Answer: Some tropical breeds of bees have adopted a nocturnal lifestyle, probably in response to the dangers and availability of resources of the tropical rainforests where they live. In contrast to European honey bees , Africanized honey bees can see under the light of a full moon and have been known to forage under these light conditions. Specialist in nocturnal vision Eric Warrant at Lund University in Sweden points out that "at light levels at which we are nearly blind, our cats are out stalking prey, and moths are flying agilely between flowers. . . . The same is true of an enormous variety of animals inhabiting the eternal darkness of the deep sea." Most of the animals in the world are primarily active in dim light, and research by Warrant and others has demonstrated that many of them see quite well. William Wcislo and his colleagues at the Smithsonian Tropical Research Institute in Panama observed that, although the light intensity at night may be as much as one hundred million times dimmer than daylight, the nocturnal sweat bees *Megalopta genalis* and *M. ecuadoria* have evolved a visual system that enables them to identify visual landmarks and navigate complex terrain in darkness. Their vision is only about thirty times more sensitive than that of diurnal bees, but specialized areas have been identified in the brains of these bees that seem to have the capacity to intensify the received images, and this may be what enables them to see well enough to forage at night (see color plate B).

Question 5: How does the queen control the hive?

Answer: The queen controls reproduction in the hive, and through that action she exerts a lot of pressure on what the workers decide to do, but she does not make the day-to-day decisions of the workers. Their behavior is influenced by the concurrent decisions of nest mates as well as by the impact of the environment outside the nest.

Queen substance is a pheromone, from the Greek *phero*, meaning "to bear," and *hormone*. Pheromones are chemical bouquets that trigger natural, behavioral responses in other individuals of the same species. Queen substance, also known as queen mandibular pheromone (QMP), is produced by the mandibular glands in the head of the queen honey bee once she has mated and is laying eggs. QMP is one of many compounds used for chemical communication within the colony (see chapter 3, question 6: How do bees communicate?). Workers smell the queen substance when they lick her body in the course of attending to her needs, and it gets passed around the colony as the bees touch each other. Because her pheromone is unique and distinct within the colony, it helps keep the colony integrated and centered around the queen as long as she is reproductively viable and the colony is healthy.

Among other effects, QMP suppresses the development of the workers' ovaries and inhibits them from rearing new queens. It signals to them, in combination with a chemical marker the queen deposits on her eggs and the presence of an adequate number of larvae, that the queen's egg laying and brood development is going well, and it influences the workers to exercise reproductive self-restraint. In the European honey bee colonies that they studied, Madeleine Beekman and Benjamin Oldroyd found that approximately 1 percent of the workers had active ovaries and were able to lay eggs. Somehow their ovaries had become activated despite all the cues to the contrary, but if they actually produced eggs, the eggs would most likely be removed, destroyed, or eaten by other workers because they lacked the queen's mark.

Christina Grozinger and her collaborators working on the Honey Bee Genome Project studied the role of QMP on gene expression, and they determined that exposure to QMP leads to direct changes in gene expression in the brains of honey bee workers. They reported that QMP consistently activates a group of genes that regulate nursing behavior and represses the activity of genes that regulate foraging activity, suggesting that QMP may delay behavioral maturation (from nurse to forager) by its effect on these groups of genes. In related research, Vanina Vergoz and colleagues identified a queen mandibular pheromone that prevents young bees from learning when to sting and has the effect of keeping them in close contact with their queen. When the bees are about three weeks old and have become mature enough to leave the hive and begin foraging, the pheromone wears off and they learn how to defend themselves. This pioneering area of research will undoubtedly lead to additional discoveries about pheromonal control of behavior in bees.

As the queen ages, her pheromone production starts to flag, her egg laying slows down, and she begins to lose reproductive control of the hive. If the queen dies or is removed from the colony, her absence is quickly noted and the behavior of the workers changes rapidly. When queen substance is scarce or is missing from a colony, the workers know that it is time to start constructing queen cells in order to rear another queen as a replacement.

There is one area where new research has established that the queen does not control the hive, as was previously thought. Andres Pierce and Lee Lewis, working with Stanley Schneider at the University of North Carolina at Charlotte, observed that colony reproduction, which involves the process of swarming and supercedure (replacing the queen), is regulated mainly by older workers rather than by the queen. In their words, the queen is relegated to the role of "passive egg layer whose own behavior is programmed, with changes dictated by signals delivered by older workers" in the form of piping and vibration signals (see chapter 3, question 6: How do bees communicate? and chapter 3, question 8: What is piping behavior?). During the two- to three-week period before swarming, older workers signal to the queen and the rest of the colony that it is time to swarm. With the queen in a passive role, they come to a group decision on a new place to locate the nest, and then they arouse the queen and the bees in the swarm and lead them all to their new home, where the queen resumes her reproductive responsibilities (see chapter 8, question 2 : What is swarming?).

Question 6: What is meant by "balling" the queen?

Answer: Bees may be hostile to a queen because she is a stranger to the hive that has been inserted by the beekeeper to replace an old queen, or she may be an old queen that is no longer laying enough eggs to meet the needs of the colony. In that situation, they will cluster around her in a ball that can be as large as three inches in diameter. Unless the queen is rescued by the beekeeper (either by using smoke or by dipping the ball in water) she will be smothered, overheated, or stung to death. To avoid this attack, beekeepers have developed various methods to safely introduce a new queen into an existing hive in order to make sure she is accepted (see chapter 11, question 9: Can the beekeeper put a new queen in the hive if the old one dies?).

Question 7: What is honeycomb?

Answer: Honeycomb is a hexagonal lattice of a single layer of relatively equal-sized cells in which nectar, honey, and pollen are stored and which contain the colony's eggs and developing brood. Made of beeswax, the walls of the comb are thin and translucent, but the wax can support thirty times its own weight. In 1999, Thomas Hales at the University of Michigan proved mathematically that this design is the most economical way to store the maximum amount of honey while using the least amount of beeswax for construction, although this idea was first hypothesized by Greek mathematician Pappus of Alexandria (A.D. 290–350). The sheet of wax that forms the base of the comb hangs vertically from the ceiling of the nest, and the cells fit together snugly and are arranged horizontally so their contents don't spill out, conserving space and maximizing storage capacity.

Stephen Pratt, now on the faculty at Arizona State University, explored the question of how a group of thousands of worker bees with limited information can proceed to build a pattern of comb that is best suited to the needs of the entire colony. What are the signals and cues that guide their collective decision making? After a swarm settles in a new nest site there is an initial surge of comb construction to provide cells for new brood and food storage (see chapter 8, question 2: What is swarming?). It might seem advantageous to build a lot of comb early in the season so that the colony can take advantage of surges in the flow of nectar due robust blooming conditions. Having empty cells can be an advantage, since if there is a shortage of storage space, foraging will have to slow down while storer bees search for places to deposit the high volume of nectar that is being collected. Construction uses up a great deal of the colony's energy resources as the builders must gorge on stored sugar supplies in order to produce wax with which to build the comb, so simply building lots of comb to be ready for a high volume of nectar is not necessarily an economical solution.

According to Pratt's observations, the winning strategy is for additional comb to be added in "pulses" throughout the nectar-gathering season, depending variably on several factors: adequate nutrition in young bees in order to promote normal wax gland development, the presence of a queen, the rate of the daily nectar flow into the colony, and the amount of empty comb that is available. How all of these factors are synthesized by the bees into a building plan and appropriate individual construction activity still remains to be discovered.

Question 8: What is propolis?

Answer: Propolis is a resinous plant substance that ranges in color from red to brownish yellow, depending on the location, season, and species of bee that collects it. Bees gather this resinous material from buds and from sap and gum on trees and use it in their hives. It is sticky when warm and brittle when it is cold.

Some breeds of honey bee are known to use large amounts of propolis, but other breeds that do not gather it are favored by beekeepers because it makes tending the beehives less cumbersome and sticky. Some stingless (*meliponid*) bees gather plant resins and mix them with the wax that they produce, creating a material called *cerumen* with the consistency of earwax. Propolis is also mixed with other substances like mud, plant matter, or even animal feces. This material is called *batumen* and it serves to strengthen and seal the nest cavity, providing extra protection that is especially important in the tropical areas where stingless bees live because of the multitude of ants and other predators that are ever ready to steal a meal of sugar or brood.

Traditional bee literature explains that bees use propolis to close gaps in the hive that let in cold air. These gaps are called *bee spaces;* if they are less than three-sixteenths of an inch, they will be filled in with propolis, and if they are wider than five-sixteenths of an inch, they will be filled in with comb. New research suggests that bees thrive with increased ventilation, and it seems that propolis may be more important in reinforcing the structure of the hive and making the hive more defensible. Bees have also been known to use propolis and wax to entomb the carcass of an intruder (like a mouse) that has died after breaking into the hive during the winter. Normally, bees carry waste out of the hive, but because a mouse is too large to remove from the hive, they effectively mummify it.

Propolis is marketed for human consumption in health food stores and by practitioners of Chinese traditional medicine, ayurveda, and homeopathy. Its chemical composition varies significantly depending on its source, and no consistent benefits have been clinically proven that are applicable to all propolis. Most of the traditional uses have not been clinically evaluated, but it may have some local antibiotic and antifungal properties. It is used to treat burns, and some feel it protects against dental caries, gingivitis, and canker sores. Beekeepers have been known to keep a piece in their mouth as a remedy for a sore throat.

Question 9: What is a brood comb?

Answer: The first three weeks of a bee's life are spent in the brood comb, give or take a few days. Usually in the lower part of the nest, this is the area where beeswax cells have been prepared to receive the eggs laid by the queen. This comb does not differ in its construction or initial appearance from the comb where the honey is made and stored. As the bees use the combs, the wax takes on the color of the nectar, pollen, and propolis that the bees collect and distribute, and it darkens after it is used repeatedly for brood rearing. While it remains clean, it can absorb the odors and chemicals present in the hive.

The temperature in the brood area needs to be kept within a very specific range in order for the brood to develop normally from egg to larvae to pupae to adult (see chapter 2, question 1: How does a honey bee develop from an egg to an adult?). During the warm weather when there is plenty of nectar, a healthy queen may lay as many as two thousand eggs each day, so there is a lot of activity in this area when so many bees a day emerge from their eggs and need to be fed. Conditions may become so crowded that the queen does not have room to lay sufficient eggs, and this may trigger swarming preparations (see chapter 8, question 2: What is swarming?).

Question 10: Is there a yearly cycle in the hive?

Answer: Honey bee colonies are perennial, so they normally live year round, attuned to the environment and totally dependent on the seasons. Their activities are limited by temperature because honey bees do not fly when the temperature is below about 45 degrees Fahrenheit (7 degrees Celsius). This physiological limitation corresponds to the growing season of the flowers that bees rely on for food, meaning that they are able to fly when food is available.

During the winter, bees stop foraging when nectar is no longer available. They depend on stored honey to sustain them through the cold weather, and they cluster together to stay warm. Most species have evolved responses that permit them to survive times of famine, and bees are no exception; they switch resources from reproduction to basic maintenance of the body. The queen stops laying eggs during the late fall and early winter so there are no larvae to attend. The bees' metabolism slows down, allowing them to minimize energy consumption when supplies are scarce. On nice days, bees emerge from the nest to get rid of wastes, but generally they stay relatively quiet until the spring arrives.

By some time in the very early spring, the queen begins laying eggs (brood production), as many as several hundred each day as long as there are ample supplies of honey and pollen remaining in the nest's storage cells and there are environmental signals that fresh supplies will soon become available as the flowers begin to come into bloom and there are enough workers to keep the eggs warm. If food is scarce, her egg-laying activity level is reduced, creating an ongoing seasonal balance between the food supply and the numbers of eggs, larvae, and pupae.

Assuming the queen is healthy as the warm weather sets in, the bees will become very active, filling the storage cells with nectar, attending to the brood, and carrying out all the normal activities of the colony. The colony population needs to be big enough to exploit the riotous blooms of spring flowers when the nectar flow reaches its maximum. The growth rate of the colony during the spring may be quite fast, and if the colony is tended by an attentive beekeeper, the colony can simply grow into the new spaces the beekeeper adds to the nest. An unattended nest may swarm if they have overgrown the available space. With a reduced population after the swarm departs and with a new queen at the reproductive helm, the colony begins to grow in number again (see chapter 8, question 2: What is swarming?). In the fall, brood production drops off and the foragers begin to prepare the nest to survive the upcoming winter, maximizing the honey stores needed to sustain the bees when the flowers are gone.

Question 11: What happens if the bees run out of honey?

Answer: It is not a satisfying answer, but "it depends" is the most accurate. If a colony is being tended by a watchful bee-keeper, the colony should not run out of honey. If honey stores are low, the beekeeper can provide honey or sugar syrup to help the bees get through the period of dearth. Feeding bees is a necessary activity in the late winter and early spring in some parts of the country, especially if the beekeeper harvests honey too late in the season, depleting the honey stored for the winter. If the colony is in a natural cavity and it runs out of honey, the bees will not be able to withstand cold temperatures. Without that source of energy to generate metabolic heat to maintain a warm enough temperature in the nest, the bees will die.

SIX

Bees at Work

Question 1: Why do bees pollinate flowers?

Answer: Bees really don't intend to pollinate flowers, although pollination benefits them because it creates seeds that will make more flowers that will provide them with a continuing nectar flow in the future. Pollen transfer is passive; unless the bee is deliberately collecting pollen to take to the nest, the pollen a bee carries from one flower to another has been deposited by the plant on her back or in another place where she was unable to remove it when she instinctively groomed herself to eliminate dust and debris. As bees go from flower to flower collecting nectar, some of the collected pollen is inadvertently deposited on the stigma of a flower of the same species, resulting in cross-pollination.

At certain times when there is a large amount of brood in the colony, honey bees' primary goal is to actively collect pollen for larval food, storing the pollen on their hind legs on dense hairs referred to as a *pollen basket* (see this chapter, question 8: Do bees ever stop collecting nectar?). These hairs surround a groove, on the external hind tibia, that creates an elongated cup-like surface where the pollen sits. Bees are able to move some of the passively collected pollen into the pollen baskets, and once the pollen is packed into the transport structures, it is no longer available for pollination and is carried back to the nest.

Fig. 19. A worker honey bee showing her specialized leg anatomy for carrying pollen. The arrow points to the corbiculum, or pollen basket. *(Drawing by Julie L. Dlugos.)*

Lawrence Harder and James Thomson describe flowers that have a dispensing schedule, requiring bees to visit more frequently because the flower's structure allows only a limited amount of pollen to be obtained in each visit. This increases the likelihood of passive transfer of at least some pollen instead of larger amounts being actively removed to provide larval food or lost to in-flight grooming.

Question 2: Which crops are pollinated by bees?

Answer: More than one hundred crop species in the United States rely to some degree on bee pollination, and these crops constitute approximately one-third of the American diet, in-

Pollination

Pollination is the process by which male and female chromosome-carrying cells (gametes) reach each other and fuse (fertilization), enabling a plant to bear fruit and reproduce. The vast majority of all plants are pollinated by living organisms, a process called *biotic* pollination. *Entomophily* is pollination by an insect. In addition to bees, moths, butterflies, wasps, ants, beetles, and flies are also insect pollinators. Pollination specifically by bees is called *melittophily*, although it is hardly a commonly used term. Honey bees and, to a lesser extent, other species of bees accomplish the majority of biotic pollination. Approximately three quarters of the over 250,000 species of flowering plants in the United States rely on mobile animal partners for pollination.

Because most bees carry an electrostatic charge that attracts lightweight particles, when they collect nectar from a flower their hairs rub against the plant's anthers and inadvertently collect the fine, dust-like grains of pollen containing the male gametes. When a foraging bee flies from flower to flower, some of the pollen grains that have been deposited on the bee will be brushed off and deposited onto the receptive female portion (the stigma) of a plant of the same species, usually resulting in fertilization. Sometimes, the goal of the bees is to collect pollen, and some species even moisten their pollen loads with nectar or oil to make it easier to transport (see this chapter, question 7: Do bees ever stop collecting nectar?). The fact that pollen transfer occurs is strictly inadvertent.

Some plants only offer nectar and pollen at specific times of the day, and many species of bees learn to adapt their foraging to the availability of their local flowers. Bees have a good sense of time, which makes it possible for them to synchronize their foraging with the plants' cycle. Because most bees tend to exhibit "floral constancy," which means that they show a preference for going from flower to flower of the same or similar species, the pollen carrying structures (usually hairs) in

(continued)

different bee species are modified according to the location of the pollen within their preferred flowers and the particular characteristics of the pollen they typically carry.

Some plants need to be vibrated in order to release pollen, and some bees oblige by grasping the anthers of the flower and shivering their flight muscles. This is called buzz pollination, and bumblebees pollinate many plants in this way, including tomatoes, raspberries, currants, oilseed rape (the source of canola oil), field beans, and many wildflowers. In addition to releasing the pollen, all that vibrating elevates the temperature of the bee, making flight easier on a cool morning. Some bees milk the anthers, grasping them near their base with the mandibles and pulling up. Biting the anthers is another way to release the pollen, and some flowers have trigger hairs that the bees need to trip before the pollen is released. There are even bees that collect pollen from the body of another bee, and there are bees with better-than-normal vision, due to enlarged ocelli, that are able to forage in low light.

Vertebrate pollination (zoophily) is primarily accomplished by hummingbirds and bats. There is also a bird called a honeyeater, belonging to a large family found mainly in Australia and New Guinea and in some Pacific islands, on which many plants in that area depend for pollination. The honey possum, found in parts of Western Australia, is a tiny nocturnal marsupial that weighs about half as much as a mouse, and its diet consists only of nectar and pollen. It has a very long tail that it uses like an extra hand when it climbs to reach nectar sources. Other vertebrates that are occasional or accidental pollinators include other birds, monkeys, marsupials, lemurs, bears, rabbits, deer, rodents, and lizards. Ninety-eight percent of the remaining plant species, especially grain crops, are pollinated by wind (anemophily), and a few aquatic plants release their gametes directly into the water, which transports them to a female plant (hydrophily). Flowers in the violet family are self-fertilizing, as are many other plants; some plants, like the dandelion, don't require pollination because they produce a seed that already contains male and female gametes.

cluding the majority of high-value crops like fruits, vegetables, and nuts. Specifically, honey bees' pollination activities are important for almonds, apples, blackberries, blueberries, melons, cherries, peaches, pears, nectarines, cucumbers, cranberries, and soybeans. Honey bees pollinate the bulk of these crops, which are worth more than fifteen billion dollars to the U.S. economy, and they also contribute indirectly to the production of meat, milk, and cheese because they pollinate food crops used for livestock.

Bumble bees pollinate 10 to 15 percent of all the crops grown in the United States, particularly crops raised in greenhouses, including tomatoes, peppers, and strawberries. Fruits and seeds produced by insect pollination are important in the diet of about 25 percent of all birds and mammals, and bees also pollinate crops that provide shelter for birds and wild animals, and they pollinate plants that prevent erosion of the soil and keep creeks clean for aquatic life in wildlife habitats.

In Sichuan Province in China, pesticides have totally eliminated the bee population in an area that was famous for its production of pears. Rather than lose the crop, farmers in that area hand pollinate the pears. They collect pollen from the male parts of the flowers, dry it, and then climb into the pear trees and dust pollen on each flower with a feather, enabling fertilization and the production of the prized fruit.

Question 3: How do flowers attract bees?

Answer: Bees are primarily attracted to nectar-rich flowers by their color and, when they are closer, by their scent; and we know that bees and other pollinators are sensitive to the ultraviolet markings on flowers that guide them to the nectar-rich area of the flower, so they can collect the nectar in a minimum of time. Recent research has demonstrated that honey bees can learn to associate odors, colors, and patterns with food rewards, so we know that many elements go into choosing rewarding nectar sources. Bees will even locate nectar sources on a terrace in an urban high-rise; they have been seen as high as the

How Do Plants Attract Bees for Pollination?

Flowers offer a variety of cues to signal that they have tasty and energizing rewards for bees and other pollinators. Bright colors and ultraviolet patterns that can be seen from a distance, attractive chemical bouquets that can be perceived when the pollinator comes closer, and tactile cues that offer sensory stimulation when the flower is touched, all are part of a plant's repertoire to ensure that its pollen gets transported to another plant so that fertilization can occur. The size of the flower, the depth of its corolla tubes, and the viscosity and composition of its nectar are the more subtle qualities that focus some plants on particular pollinators.

When scientists experimentally modify plant characteristics, they often see a change in pollinator visitation. One such study involved the bee-pollinated monkeyflower *Mimulus lewisii*, a pink flower that is low in carotenoid pigments and has a wide corolla and a small volume of nectar, and the hummingbird-pollinated monkeyflower *Mimulus cardinali*, a red flower with a narrow corolla tube and a large nectar pool. When cross-breeding and genetic manipulation increased the concentration of carotenoid pigments in hybrids of the two species, bee visitation was reduced by a striking 80 percent. When they experimentally increased nectar production, hummingbird visitation doubled. These results focus on the adaptation of plants to the pollinators in their habitat and also nicely demonstrate that pollinators have strong preferences with regard to color and nectar reward. To some degree there is convergent evolution, a co-construction or mutual adaptation to each other's needs and attributes.

And then there are some plants that have more unusual strategies for attracting pollinators, even some plants that can't offer a nectar reward but still manage to be seductive. The primary alternative strategies used by these plants to attract bees are sex and heat.

When orchids in the genus *Ophrys* are in bloom, they ap-

How Do Plants Attract Bees for Pollination?

pear to be covered with female bees and they give off a chemical bouquet that is similar to the female's sexual attractant (pheromone). The lip (labellum) of the flower is shaped and colored to resemble a particular species of female insect, and each different species of the orchid attracts males of a particular species of bee. A male bee lands on the orchid's labellum and tries to mate with it (pseudocopulation), and in the process he gets pollen stuck to his head, which he transfers to the next flower. Mission accomplished.

There are certain large *Oncocyclus* irises that grow in the Middle East, and these flowers have no nectar to offer, so they don't attract diurnal pollinators, but they do attract solitary male bees at dusk by offering a warm place to sleep within the flower. Pollen from the flowers was found on almost 40 percent of the males that had slept in the floral suntraps, supporting the conclusion that fertilization of these irises is dependent on their night sheltering of solitary male bees. In the laboratory, bumblebees *Bombus terrestris* were observed to prefer warmer artificial flowers to unheated artificial flowers containing the same nectar reward if they could tell the difference by color. When all the flowers were the same color and only some were heated, the bees were unsuccessful in reliably finding the warm flowers.

Plants develop a variety of qualities to entice pollinators, either by fair means or foul. Animals have their wiles, too, but when they pretend to offer food or sex, their goal is usually to kill the pollinator, rather then take advantage of its services (see chapter 3, question 14: Do bees ever get fooled by predators?). Seduction is not unique in the environment of the bee—it exists for everyone, many other insects as well as birds and other animals and, of course, humans. So when you smell something delicious or see something that looks irresistible, remember—it's a jungle out there.

thirty-fourth floor in Manhattan by co-author Carol Butler. Bees learn the location of rewarding food sites and will return to them regularly—terraces are no exception.

Question 4: Are there any flowers that bees prefer or avoid?

Answer: In his research, Cornell University scientist Thomas Seeley found that honey bees focus on flowers with higher concentrations of nectar when there is plenty of nectar available, but they forage among a wider range of flowers when nectar is in short supply. Nectar volume, composition, and concentration vary among different species of plants and can wax and wane at different times in the flowering season of the plant and at different times of the day. Seeley's research indicates that most nectars are somewhere in the range of 15 to 65 percent sugar, and honey bees tend to prefer nectar high in sucrose over glucose and fructose. Theodora Petanidou analyzed the nectars of seventy-three plant species in the Mediterranean area, and she found that summer-flowering plants had a higher percentage of sucrose in their nectar, which goes along with the general tendency of sugar concentrations to be highest in sunny areas. She also confirmed that bees (and wasps) prefer high-sucrose nectars, which facilitates sharing the resources in the habitat because flies, beetles, and butterflies prefer lower sucrose nectars.

Hannelle Human and Susan Nicholson studied these variations in *Aloe greatheadii* var. *davyana,* a preferred nectar source in South Africa, and they found that the volume and concentration of the nectar remained relatively the same during the day, despite wide shifts in temperature and humidity. Jacobus Biesmeijer and his colleagues found that stingless bees preferred nectar at a 60 percent concentration over less concentrated sources, and in their experiments *Melipona beecheii* completely ignored 20 percent solutions. The bees' own physical characteristics (morphology) apparently play a role in the choice of nec-

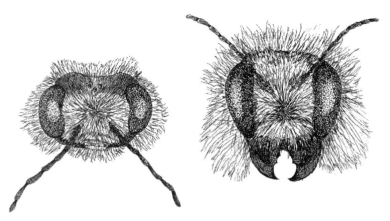

Fig. 20.   The head of the red mason bee, *Osmia rufa,* introduced to North America from England, showing long body hairs and large jaws, or mandibles (*on right*). The illustration on the *left* shows an unusually shaped head that accommodates the muscles that work the large jaws. (*Drawing by John F. Cullum.*)

tar sources for the stingless bees studied. *Melipona beecheii* has a yellowish body and these bees were observed to prefer sunny patches, while *M. fasciata* with its dark brown body preferred shady locations. Mason bees, *Chalicodoma sicula,* studied by Pat Willmer in an arid area of Israel preferred more dilute nectar, and in that habitat collecting adequate amounts of water from flowers was more vital even than the energy reward of nectar.

There are certain flowers that bees learn to avoid. Gustavo Romero and Craig Nelson studied a certain female orchid, *Catasetum ochraceum,* which receives pollen from a bee and then swells and closes up, creating a very limited opportunity for fertilization. Male flowers of this species compete to be the one that fertilizes the female by rapidly heaping sticky sacs of pollen onto the back of any bee that visits. The large pollen sacs can weigh up to a quarter of the bee's bodyweight, and after one such experience, bees avoid male *Catasetum* and visit only females. Some related species exhibit similar learning behavior.

Some floral nectars contain toxins, secondary compounds such as alkaloids that are produced by plants to defend themselves against nectar thieves such as ants and other species that compete with pollinators for the resources of the flower. The toxins can produce erratic movement or loss of balance in the ants, and Andrew Stephenson reported that he twice observed skippers landing on innocent-looking and accessible *Catalpa speciosa* flowers, probing for nectar, and then dropping comatose from the flowers. David Rhoades and Jas Bergdahl have described some plant toxins that can incapacitate or even kill nectaring bees and will make any honey produced from the nectar toxic to humans. Some "mad" honey made from certain nectars can be toxic to humans but doesn't seem to affect the bees (see chapter 7, question 8: Can honey be toxic to humans?).

Question 5: How do farmers make sure there are enough bees to pollinate their crops?

Answer: In rural areas, local bees pollinate the flowers during the growing season, rotating from one species to another as each one comes into bloom and finding enough nectar to sustain the colony. Smaller farmers often arrange with local beekeepers to locate their hives on or near the farmer's property to improve their access to the pollinators. Farmers who want to encourage bee pollination try to provide continuous blooming by planting a variety of native species so the local bees can flourish, and they limit or stop the use of pesticides and lawn herbicides.

Huge commercial farms that grow only one crop (monoculture) cannot attract enough local bees to provide sufficient pollination when their crop is in bloom, and when the blooming season is over the farm has nothing growing to provide forage to sustain the bees. This has become an environmental issue as the number of commercial monoculture farms has increased, and the solution has taken the form of commercial beekeepers who migrate around the country with trucks full of hives, moving their bees to wherever there is a seasonal crop that needs pollinating. Commercial pollination has become a $14.6 billion business, according to figures obtained in 2008. Blue bottle flies and leaf cutter bees are also raised and sold for managed pollination.

When bees are rearing large quantities of brood, they temporarily focus on gathering pollen to provide protein for the larvae (see chapter 2, question 2: What do larvae eat?). Although the transfer of pollen is always unintentional, a honey bee that is deliberately gathering pollen is up to ten times more efficient as a pollinator than one that is primarily gathering nectar, so commercial beekeepers try to manage their hives so that the bees are in this pollen-gathering state when their "money" crops are in bloom.

Close to one million honey bee hives are needed in California in the spring when the almond orchards are in bloom. The apple trees in New York require about thirty thousand hives, and the blueberry crop in Maine requires about fifty thousand hives each year. Other crops that are raised on monoculture farms that import beehives are cucumbers, melons, squash, blueberries, and strawberries. Tomatoes and other crops raised primarily in greenhouses use bumble bees for buzz pollination (see this chapter, question 8: What is buzz pollination?).

Question 6: How much weight in pollen can a bee carry?

Answer: A worker honey bee has rows of hairs on the inner surface of her hind leg which serve as a pollen basket. She has a structure on her leg that serves as a comb, and she uses it to scrape pollen from the body hairs and to transport the pollen grains to the basket. In other bees, such as the Megachilid, or leaf cutters, the females have special pollen hairs (scopal) on the underside of the abdomen that are very effective at attracting pollen, which they transport to their nest. A load of pollen carried by a bee is not as heavy as the weight of an average nectar load.

Typical studies, such as one conducted by Athole Marshall, Terry Michaelson-Yeates, and Ingrid Williams, tend to measure how far bees carry the pollen, patterns of pollen deposition, and the rate of successful pollination, but we know of no contemporary studies weighing honey bee loads.

In Gustavo Romero and Craig Nelson's research on pollination of *Catasetum ochraceum* orchids, they reported that the flowers released their pollen sacs onto the backs of visiting "orchid" bees (also called euglossine bees) and that the pollen load could weigh as much as a quarter of the bee's known bodyweight (they determined this by weighing the pollen sacs). The bees reacted to this experience by becoming averse to visiting these orchids again, suggesting that the bees found carrying this amount of pollen to be uncomfortable or distasteful.

Manuela Giovanetti and Eloisa Lasso actually weighed bees to determine how much pollen they carried. Their subjects were 192 female communal bees, *Andrena agilissima,* in Tuscany, Italy, in the area of Isola d'Elba. The bees weighed from 67 to 127 mg, with an average weight of 95.75 mg (compared to a honey bee that weighs, on average, about 190 mg). Despite the range in bodyweight, there was no relationship between how much pollen the bee transported and her size. The pollen load carried by each bee varied from 6.3 percent to 37.5 percent of a bee's body weight.

The process by which Giovanetti and Lasso weighed the bees is fascinating. After each bee was captured, she was placed in a glass cup which was then put into a cooler with ice for about five minutes in order to temporarily immobilize her. Then each bee was transferred to an empty transparent pill capsule that prevented her from moving and losing pollen. After the bee plus its load was weighed on a precise digital scale, she was transferred to a shaded box for about half an hour's recovery time, during which she groomed herself and removed any pollen grains. Then an investigator gently pressed on the abdomen of the bee, causing her to regurgitate any nectar in her crop. The nectar's weight was estimated, and then the bee was re-weighed without any load.

Question 7: Do bees ever stop collecting nectar?

Answer: The amount of nectar that honey bees collect varies from season to season and on the time of day. When there is a large amount of brood in the colony, foragers concentrate on collecting pollen to feed the larvae (see chapter 2, question 2: What do larvae eat?); they collect just enough nectar to supply themselves with energy.

Bees don't collect nectar at a constant rate throughout the day. Manuela Giovanetti and Eloisa Lasso found that although pollen loads were fairly constant, the amount of nectar the bees transported increased in the afternoon, as did the sugar concentration stored in their crop. The number of bees carrying nectar increased as the day progressed; in the morning only 2 to 12 percent of the bees collected had nectar in their crop, while in the afternoon from 45 to 89 percent of the bees collected were carrying nectar.

Sometimes, when the nectar flow rate is high, the bees will collect more nectar than they can use, and the honeycomb cells become filled faster than the bees can build new comb. Beekeepers describe a colony in this state as being "honey bound," and when this occurs, the workers will slow down their nectar collection.

Question 8: What is buzz pollination?

Answer: The flowers of some plants, such as tomatoes and other plants in the Nightshade, or Solanaceae, family contain no nectar but do produce pollen. They need to be shaken to release the pollen, and at one time this was usually done by humans or, in the wild, by the wind. Farmers have realized that bumble bees and other sonicating bees (bees that produce resonant vibrations) are extremely efficient as "buzz" pollinators, and imported bumble bees are now widely used as the primary pollinators for greenhouse tomatoes and other self-fertilizing fruit such as kiwis (also known as Chinese gooseberries), rape, field beans, raspberries, and currants. To release the pollen in these flowers, bumble bees grasp the tubular anthers of the plant containing the pollen and rapidly vibrate the flight muscles of the thorax, causing the pollen to be dislodged. The pollen is carried on their hairs to the stigma of another plant, resulting in fertilization.

Bees and Honey in Judaism

"The true and righteous words and judgments of the Lord are said to be sweeter than honey" (Psalm 19:10; Psalm 119:103; Ezekiel 3:1–3; Revelation 10:9–11). Honey is consumed as a symbol of the New Year in the Jewish tradition. On the holiday Rosh Hashanah, bread and apple slices are dipped into honey and eaten to bring a sweet new year. In what is now the Republic of Georgia, formerly part of Russia, honey was part of a Jewish marriage custom. The doorposts of newly married couples were smeared with butter and honey to symbolize a sweet and prosperous match. Beeswax candles are important in the Jewish faith because the flames of beeswax are considered to be pure and worthy of their role in worship. In "Prophets," sugar is referred to as dry honey.

In Hebrew, the name for a bee is *dbure*, from the root *dbr*, meaning "speech." The woman's name Deborah comes from the Hebrew word *Devorah*, which means "honey bee" and derives from the Hebrew word *debesh*.

Question 9: How do bees make beeswax?

Answer: Wax is produced by young adult bees that are between twelve and seventeen days old. When wax is needed in the colony, they prepare themselves to secrete the wax by gorging either on nectar that has been stored in a cell in the colony or on sugar syrup that is provided by the beekeeper. They then rest for up to twenty-four hours while their bodies metabolize the wax, and then each bee approaches the comb and searches for a place that needs work. She has eight tiny slits on her abdomen, and tiny, moist scales of wax emerge from these openings, secreted by special glands that gradually atrophy when the bee gets older and begins foraging (see figure 6 in chapter 1).

Bees and Honey in the Bible

Honey is mentioned sixty-one times in the New King James version of the Bible, symbolizing sweetness, prosperity, purity, and eloquence. Milk and honey were considered rich and pure enough to be food for the gods, and the Promised Land is frequently described as a "land flowing with milk and honey." John the Baptist, the first-century Jewish preacher and ascetic, is described as eating only "locusts and wild honey," symbolically indicating that he is a man of God (Matthew 3:4; Mark 1:6).

Jesus proved to his frightened disciples that he was truly resurrected and human by eating a piece of broiled fish and some honeycomb (Luke 24:42). St. Ambrose taught that the church is a beehive and the bees are the faithful, diligently storing up treasure or honey in heaven, and St. Ambrose is represented in the Roman Catholic Church as the patron saint of beekeepers. According to the Golden Legend, St. Ambrose's father predicted his eventual eloquence when he discovered the sleeping infant's head covered with a swarm of bees. Beehives are also used in the Bible to represent peaceful, wisely ruled communities, nations, and monasteries which are governed by a single head. The Bible warns that Jesus' words may sting the sinner.

The pleasant words of humans are compared to the health-giving honeycomb (Proverbs 16:24). A sweet-talking person's lips "drip as the honeycomb," even if they are the deceitful words of a harlot (Song of Solomon 4:11; Proverbs 5:3). Proverbs warns against too much sweetness, saying, "Have you found honey? Eat only as much as you need, lest you be filled with it and vomit" (Proverbs 25:16).

Because the queen bee can be observed laying eggs continuously without any sign of mating, bees were once believed to be born from unfertilized eggs, and so became symbols of chastity, moral purity, and the Virgin Mary. The alleged

(continued)

Bees and Honey in the Bible, *continued*

sexual purity of bees made beeswax suitable for candles to burn in religious ceremonies.

On the negative or cautionary side, swarms of bees and the danger of their attacks are mentioned in Psalms 118:12 ("They surrounded me like bees"). In Isaiah 7:18 the "fly" and the "bee" are personifications, respectively, of the Egyptians and the Assyrians, inveterate enemies of Israel.

Samson found a "swarm of bees and honey" in the carcass of a lion he had slain (Judges 14:8), and it led him to pose this riddle: "Out of the eater came something to eat, and out of the strong came something sweet" (Judges 14:14).

Using a rear leg with spiky tongs, she takes each flake one at a time, chews it in her mouth for a few minutes to soften it, and places it on the honeycomb cell. Then each added bit of wax is smoothed and polished, and she moves along to another spot that needs her attention. Beeswax is composed of fatty acids, alcohol, hydrocarbons, and other substances; it is white when the bees first secrete it, but it gradually yellows and darkens. In the brood area it can look brown to black because it incorporates pollen, oil, and propolis residue from the larval food, plus cocoons from the bee brood.

Depending on a variety of factors, such as the breed of bee, the quantity and quality of honey, and the stressors in the colony, anywhere from four to twelve pounds of honey must be eaten in order to produce one pound of beeswax, and that pound can create as many as thirty-five thousand cells. Another way to conceptualize this is that ten thousand bees can produce about one pound of beeswax in three days.

Over eight million pounds of beeswax are produced each year, mostly to be used as an ingredient in industrial lubricants, salves, ointments, furniture polish, ski wax, crayons, adhesives,

Each honey bee hive contains wooden frames filled with beeswax. The brood are in the center of the frame, while pollen and honey are stored in the peripheral areas, making a rainbow in the frame. *(Photograph by Debra Cook-Balducci.)*

B

Honey bees are very hairy insects. This bee even has hairs between the facets of her eyes. *(Photograph by Jeri Wright.)*

Megalopta genalis, a nocturnal sweat bee, has very large eyes and expanded ocelli, or simple eyes, on the top of its head. *(Photograph by Alexander T. Baugh.)*

C

Some seemingly plain flowers have hidden nectar guides that point to the location of their food rewards. Bees can see colors within the ultraviolet spectrum. We can, too, using special ultraviolet light photography that exposes the dark lines that appear on these black-eyed Susan daisies. *(Composite image created by Tom Biegalski/www.TTBphoto.com.)*

Orchid bees, like this male in the genus *Euglossa*, have very long tongues. They visit flowers for both food and floral oils, but scientists are uncertain what the males do with these scents. Orchid bees are largely restricted to the neotropics, but a small population of *Euglossa viridissima* has been identified in Dade County, Florida, USA. *(Photograph by Nicole Tharp.)*

A: Color picture of a flower (*Gelsemium sempervirens*) for human vision.
B: Photograph of the flower taken through an ultraviolet transmitting lens.
C: False color image taken through an optical device simulating bee shape and color vision.
D: A filtered image that removes facets. This image is the most accurate simulation of bee color and spatial vision that has been developed and may hold lessons for technological advances using miniaturized optics.
(*Image by Susan Williams and Adrian Dyer.*)

Food sharing, or trophallaxis, is an important part of the many social exchanges within a honey bee colony. Here, the bee at the top is feeding the bee at the bottom. (*Photograph by Debra Cook-Balducci.*)

When honey bee workers emerge from the pupal state, they chew their way out of their natal cell. The bee on the right is almost free of the wax, while the bee in the middle is still pulling her way out. The bee on the left is a full emerged, fluffy adult. (*Photograph by Joe Spencer.*)

F

The nest of a stingless bee, *Melipona beechii*, is kept under the eaves of a house in rural Honduras. Honey is harvested once a year using a side entrance that is fitted with a wooden plug. *(Photo by Elizabeth C. Evans.)*

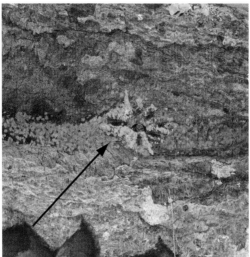

Many stingless bees close the waxy doors to their nests at night to keep marauding ants out. *Melipona beechii* is known in Honduras as *las abejas de estrella blanca,* or the "white star bees," because of the star-shaped nest entrance that is rebuilt each morning. *(Photograph by Elizabeth C. Evans.)*

Many stingless bees make their nests in the fallen branches of trees, including this species of *Melipona* from the forest around Santo Tomas, Honduras. *(Photograph by Jose Nuñez-Miño.)*

Wooden carvings with bee motifs found inside the Bee Hive House, Salt Lake City, Utah. (*Photographs by Elizabeth C. Evans.*)

Honey bee imagery is common in Salt Lake City, Utah, including on the top of the Joseph Smith Administration Building in Temple Square. (*Photograph by Elizabeth C. Evans.*)

Abandoned honey bee colonies are regularly infested with wax moths; here, pupal cases of these moths are visible on the tops of frames. *(Photograph by Elizabeth C. Evans.)*

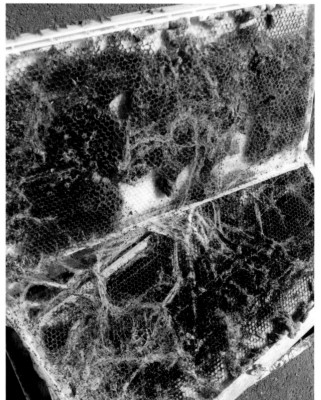

Wax moth larvae feed on the wax remains of a former honey bee colony; they leave silken trails throughout the abandoned nest. *(Photograph by Elizabeth C. Evans.)*

inks, varnish, insulation, figurines, sculptures, and, of course, candles. When purified, beeswax has a high melting point (140 degrees Fahrenheit), which has an advantage over other waxes for applications in manufacturing.

Question 10: How is beeswax used in different cultures?

Answer: Multiple cultures used beeswax to produce light or fire in the form of candles, torches, or lamps. Because of its flammability, beeswax was also a component in incendiary weapons during the Crusades of the Middle Ages and in other battles as well. Before plastic was invented, beeswax was the best method available for food storage, and it was used to seal wine casks and jars of olive oil. Cheeses, meats, and eggs were sealed or dipped in beeswax to preserve them, and wax is still used in packaging some of these foods.

The Egyptians used beeswax to create figures to be put in tombs and to make molds. Beeswax figurines thought to have magical properties were also made by Aborigines in Australia, who, like other tribal peoples in Central and South America, made these objects from the waxes within stingless bee nests. Beeswax effigies were used in Roman times for various rituals, including funerals, and wax models were created for the study of human anatomy throughout European cultures.

The "lost wax" process of metal casting for sculpture was developed in ancient times, and according to Eva Crane, the process was widely used at one time throughout Europe, Asia, Africa, and the Americas. It is still used today by some sculptors and in commercial applications. In the lost wax method, layered wax is used to retain the impression of an image and then the wax serves as a mold and is finally melted away, yielding a sculpture cast in bronze or another material. Beeswax was also used in Egypt to embalm corpses, something bees do with propolis as well (see chapter 5, question 8: What is

Fig. 21. Early Egyptians used a complex pictographic writing system that in-cluded both logograms (where one sign represents a word, such as an owl rep-resenting an owl) and phonograms (where one sign represented one or more consonantal sounds, such as an owl representing the consonant *m*). The bee glyph, pictured here from the Temple of Horus at Edfu, Egypt, could function as a pictogram meaning "bee" or "honey" or as a phonogram for the sounds *bt;* early on, it also came to be a symbol for the kingdom of Lower Egypt, meaning "he of the bee," or ruler of Lower Egypt. *(Photo by Matthew B. Heintzelman.)*

propolis?). Roman historians of the fifth century B.C.E. described wrapping deceased royalty in cloths dipped in wax. Bodies pre-served in this way were carried in processions around the king-dom of the deceased so that their followers could pay their last respects.

The Romans used beeswax as a writing surface. Messages were sent on wooden writing tablets coated with beeswax through-out the Middle Ages in Europe. The message was written in the wax with a stylus, and it could easily be erased and the tablet could be reused to write a reply. The Greeks used beeswax for decorative painting, and they mixed it with pigment to surface

Honey in Islam

The Qur'an refers to "rivers of honey pure and clear" in paradise (47:15), mentions honey as war booty (53:382), and cautions against it in the form of an intoxicating liquor "which the Yemenites used to drink" (59:631). A "gulp of honey" is valued for its healing properties (71:584), and it is specifically recommended by the Prophet Muhammed for abdominal troubles (71:588).

Aisha, one of Muhammed's wives, tells the following amusing story about how she stopped her husband from spending extra time with another of his wives (63:193). Muhammed was known to be fond of honey and sweet things to eat. After the last prayer of the day, he would customarily visit his wives and stay with one of them for the night. One evening he went to his wife Hafsa, the daughter of Umar, and stayed with her longer than usual, which made Aisha jealous. She found out that the reason Muhammed had stayed so long was that Hafsa had received a gift of a skin filled with honey, and she had made syrup from it and had given it to Muhammed to drink, which had delayed him. Aisha said, "By Allah we will play a trick on him," and she told Sada bint Zam'a, another of Muhammed's wives, that when he approached her, she should ask him if he had taken Maghafir (a bad-smelling gum). Assuming he would say "No," she was to reply, "Then what is this bad smell which I smell from you?" He hopefully would reply, "Hafsa made me drink honey syrup," in which case Sada was to respond, "Perhaps the bees of that honey had sucked the juice of the tree of Al-'Urfut, which is a foul-smelling flower." Aisha vowed that she herself would have the same conversation with him, and, indeed, they carried out their plan. And when Muhammed again went to Hafsa and she offered him more of the drink, he replied, "I am not in need of it." Upon hearing of this exchange, Sada said, "By Allah, we deprived him of it," and Aisha replied, "Keep quiet."

(continued)

Honey in Islam, *continued*

A man came to the Prophet and said, "I saw in a dream, a cloud having shade. Butter and honey were dropping from it and I saw the people gathering it in their hands, some gathering much and some a little." Abu Bakr said, "Allow me to interpret this dream." The Prophet said to him, "Interpret it." Abu Bakr said, "The cloud with shade symbolizes Islam, and the butter and honey dropping from it symbolizes the Qur'an, its sweetness dropping and some people learning much of the Qur'an and some a little (vol. 9, book 87, number 170).

walls. They also used it as a protective, water-resistant coating for boats, leather armor, and tents.

Beeswax is also an important component in the production of various dyed textiles and patterned metals or glass. Garments and decorative fabrics were marked with beeswax, which would then resist coloration by dyes or pigments. The wax-resist strategy is thought to have been initiated in India, and the techniques were passed along via the Silk Road traders.

Honey

Question 1: What is honey?

Answer: Honey is a sweet and viscous fluid that honey bees produce. Most people have a jar of honey in the kitchen, but they probably don't use it very often. In the days before the development of refined sugars, honey was of great importance because it was the primary sweetener available. Honey is *hygroscopic,* meaning it pulls moisture from the air, so baked goods made with honey tend to stay moist. This property of honey creates an unfavorable environment for bacteria and mold, drawing water from inside their cells and causing them to die of dehydration. Honey is also quite acidic, which further prevents spoilage and inhibits germs. Archaeologists have found edible honey that is over three thousand years old from the tombs of Egyptian pharaohs, and experts believe that honey had an important role in many civilizations and cultures.

Over 181 chemical substances have been identified in honey, although it varies from hive to hive, depending on the nectar source. Honey is roughly 38 percent fructose, 31 percent glucose, and may contain maltose, sucrose, and other complex carbohydrates. It usually contains vitamins B6 and C, thiamin, niacin, riboflavin, and pantothenic acid, and it may have traces of essential minerals such as calcium, copper, iron, magnesium, manganese, phosphorus, potassium, sodium, zinc, and several different amino acids. It also contains antioxidants and is fat free.

Honey that has been adequately dehydrated can be safely stored for long periods of time. However, if the air is too dry, the sugar crystals in honey can reform and give liquid honey an unappealing appearance. Luckily, crystallization can be reversed through gentle heating, which restores the liquid nature of most honeys. When honey is judged at a county or state fair, judges look for color, flavor, sugar content, as well as density, freedom from crystals, cleanliness of the honey, and neatness in the packaging.

Question 2: How does nectar become honey?

Answer: The production of honey begins when foraging bees transport nectar back to the hive that they have collected from nearby flowers. The foraging bees accumulate the nectar in a special organ called a *honey stomach,* or *crop,* without digesting it. New research conducted by Susan Nicolson and Hannelle Human in South Africa demonstrated that the sugar concentration of the nectar collected by honey bees from a local aloe plant, *Aloe greatheadii* var. *davyana,* doubled between the time the bees collected it and when they delivered it to the hive, and its volume decreased as well. This result suggests that the bees begin processing the nectar into honey immediately, regurgitating it onto their tongue and evaporating it on the flight back to the colony.

Once back in the hive, a forager bee unloads the nectar by regurgitating it drop by drop, and a food storer bee sucks up the fluid with her proboscis from the forager's mouth. As the nectar is passed between bees, the complex sugars in the nectar are converted by enzymes produced by glands inside the bees' heads into simple sugars, primarily glucose, fructose, and sucrose, which become honey.

The food storer bees deposit the honey one drop at a time into storage cells in the honeycomb until the cells are filled. Once a cell is full, workers fan it with their wings until the water content of the honey has been reduced from the nectar's original 80 percent to less than 20 percent, and then they cover the storage cell with a wax cap. The stored honey can be used to sustain the colony through the winter until foraging starts again in the spring. Honey does not spoil (but it can ferment), so if it is not used during the winter, it will provide a reserve for the colony in the early spring.

Question 3: Why are there so many different kinds of honey?

Answer: The flavor and color of honey depend on which flowers the bees have been using as a nectar source. Nectar sources vary with the blooming cycle, location, and weather, and some local beekeepers collect particular types of honey in coordination with the blooming of certain flowers that they prefer. Many beekeepers think that the best honey-making nectar comes from alfalfa, tupelo, buckwheat, clover, cotton, and orange. Beekeepers typically allow the bees to keep honey that they make from other flowers, and many hobby beekeepers don't try to label their honey based on the floral crop—they are simply happy to have a crop of naturally harvested honey. Honey of mixed floral origins is generally labeled "wildflower" honey. Natural food stores, growers, and farmers' markets typically sell honeys made from plants that grow locally, and stores in New York and elsewhere sell unusual honeys imported from Morocco, labeled carob seed, lavender, and jujube (a bitter, apple-like fruit.)

There are also different types of honey depending on how much it is processed. There is cut comb honey (cut straight from the honeycomb and bottled with the honeycomb wax), certified organic, chunk, strained or filtered, ultrafiltered, heat-treated, ultrasonicated, churned or whipped (also called honey fondant or spun honey), crystallized, and set honey. Raw honey is produced without heating, and some people consider this the tastiest type of honey available. Crystallized or whipped honey is the most preferred form of honey in many places in Europe, while Americans tend to prefer liquid honey.

Question 4: Is honey good for you?

Answer: Honey never spoils (if it is stored properly) and contains a surprisingly high level of antioxidants, non-nutritive agents that can slow destructive chemical reactions in food and animal tissues. A recent survey of a variety of monofloral honeys determined that, in general, the darker the honey, the higher the value of its antioxidant content. Buckwheat honey, one of the darkest types tested by May Berenbaum along with Steve Frankel and Gene Robinson, had the highest antioxidant content, greater than sunflower, tupelo, soybean, and clover varieties. Experiments conducted by other authors, including Nele Gheldof and colleagues, support the findings that honey should be valued because of its capacity to act as an antioxidant.

Honey is also a good source of carbohydrates to fuel aerobic exercise. According to Richard Kreider and colleagues, honey is easily digestible and its fuel is released very steadily after it is eaten, suggesting that it is an excellent way to promote sports performance and recovery. Skeptics, however, warn that honey is simply touted as a fad diet for athletes.

Bassan Zeina and colleagues state that honey is effective against a tropical, infectious parasite called *Leishmania*. In multiple studies, Mutya Subrahmanyam and colleagues indicate that mild burns healed faster when treated with honey and covered with gauze than similar burns that were treated with antibiotic creams and other dressings. Owen Moore and coauthors, however, published a meta-analysis of seven other published papers investigating honey as a burn treatment, concluding that there is a dearth of evidence about the efficacy of honey in this capacity and citing the lack of double-blind controls and poor validity testing. Many reports about medical uses of honey are anecdotal rather than being based on scientific or experimental studies; for example, in Sierra Leone, a drop of honey is put in each ear of a newborn baby to prevent infection. There is some evidence that honey may be a useful way to combat periodontal disease and gingivitis, but contrary evidence indicates that the highly acidic nature of honey makes the sugar content potentially damaging to the human mouth and teeth.

A study published in the *Archives of Pediatrics and Adolescent Medicine* in 2007 by Ian Paul and colleagues suggests that honey may be beneficial to children suffering with persistent coughs. One hundred and five symptomatic children aged two to eighteen years of age participated in the study: thirty minutes before bedtime, they were given either a dose of buckwheat honey, honey-flavored cough medicine, or no treatment. Honey was rated by the parents of the children as having provided the most symptomatic relief of the nighttime coughing and sleep difficulty. Clearly, more research is needed to establish the degree of honey's health benefits.

Question 5: What is flea honey or honeydew?

Answer: Honeydew is a sweet substance excreted by aphids, also called plant lice, which are small, soft-bodied insects. They feed on the fluids in plants using a needle-like, biting mouthpart and are considered plant pests because they can damage trees, garden flowers, or agricultural crops if their population is large. Ladybugs, also known as ladybird beetles, are frequently released on aphid-infested plants because these beetles are predatory and eat aphids.

As the aphids suck liquids from the plants, they exude drops of liquid waste called honeydew. It is a clear, sticky liquid often seen on automobiles parked under trees and on car windshields during the summer. Bees, ants, and some caterpillars sip drops of excess honeydew that the aphids excrete. Bees in habitats that have lots of aphids but few flowering plants collect the honeydew and bring it back to the hive to be made into "flea honey."

Question 6: How much work does it take for bees to make a jar of honey?

Answer: Nectar that is turned into honey is gathered by bees drop by drop. It has been estimated that bees have to visit two

Honey Hunters in Rock Art

Evidence abounds that bees have had sacred and mystical significance in cultures and religions in prehistoric, ancient, and modern times. The queen lays eggs continuously without any evidence of mating, the tiny eggs undergo complete metamorphosis, and the bees somehow create elaborate and perfect hives containing a highly desirable, sweet, and healing substance. It is truly magical.

In some cultures, a foraging bee was marked with a drop of liquid or tagged with a piece of fluff or a strand of animal hair so that a human observer could more easily follow the bee and find its nest. It was a common belief that personal cleanliness and purity, including sexual abstinence, would protect a male honey hunter from being stung.

A Mesolithic rock painting was found on a wall of Arana Cave near Valencia in eastern Spain showing two naked men collecting honey and honeycombs from a wild nest. They are depicted using a long ladder and carrying baskets or bags. The painting has been dated variously from 6000 B.C.E. to 13,000 B.C.E. and may be the oldest evidence of human interest in bees and honey to date.

Eva Crane, the leading authority on honey hunter images, has collected images from rock paintings found around the world in which bees' nests and honey hunting are represented. The differences in the size, shape, and location of the nests in the paintings are quite striking, and there is often enough resemblance to contemporary wild beehives to suggest a tentative identification of the species, thus potentially establishing its existence in a specific locale. A great deal of this rock art was found in southern Africa, but examples have also been collected from Asia, Europe, northern Africa, and Australia.

Extraordinarily clear ancient engravings and paintings on stone detailing honey being harvested from human-made hives have been found in Egypt and dated around 2400 B.C.E., and physical evidence of artificial hives made from hollow logs as well as pottery vessels, woven straw baskets, and sealed

Honey Hunters in Rock Art

honey pots were found in the graves of Tutankhamen and other pharaohs.

In 2007, archaeologists digging in the ruins of the city of Rehov in northern Israel discovered evidence of a three-thousand-year-old beekeeping industry, including what they believe are the oldest intact beehives—thirty of them, dating back to 900 B.C.E. The beehives are made of straw and un-baked clay, and they were found in orderly rows, three high, in a room that was big enough to hold one hundred hives. An altar decorated with fertility figures was found alongside the hives, suggesting that they might have served some ritual or religious function.

million flowers to obtain enough nectar to make one eight-ounce jar of honey. They have to fly approximately fifty-five thousand miles back and forth from flowers to hive to gather enough nectar for that one jar, and to make one gallon of honey they have to fly the distance to the moon and back. How much honey a hive produces varies greatly, depending on the climate, location, weather, and general health of the bees, but the amount ranges from about fifty pounds to as much as two hundred pounds in a year.

Question 7: How much honey is gathered in the United States every year?

Answer: About 150 million pounds of honey are obtained each year in the United States from commercial sources. About five hundred thousand people keep hives, and there are approximately 2.5 million colonies of bees according to the U.S. National Agricultural Statistics Service. The amount of honey that is harvested from smaller beekeeping operations and hob-byist beekeepers is impossible to estimate.

Prior to the 1980s, beekeeping was a very common hobby. Many hobbyist beekeepers lived in rural areas, and the beehives provided pollination for small gardens and local fruit orchards and supplied the household with honey and beeswax. In the 1980s, parasitic tracheal mites arrived in the United States and infested many colonies, and in the 1990s, *Varroa* mites and small hive beetles joined the party, resulting in the demise of most rural colonies (see chapter 10, question 3: What parasites and insects prey on bees?). Most beekeeping is presently being done commercially; although, with the recent interest in honey bees due to the publicity about colony collapse disorder, there is a resurgence of interest in keeping bees (see chapter 10, question 10: What is colony collapse disorder?).

In 2007, the state with the most honey-producing honey bee colonies was North Dakota, with California and South Dakota in second and third place, respectively. Kentucky had the fewest number of registered bee colonies. The greatest yield per colony was from Mississippi, but total production was highest from North Dakota, California, and South Dakota, with Florida coming in very close to the top three producers. According to the Agricultural Statistics Board of the U.S. Department of Agriculture, the total value of honey production across the United States in 2007 was $153,233,000.

Question 8: Can honey be toxic to humans?

Answer: Honey from certain flowers is called "mad" honey. It is produced when bees collect nectar from rhododendrons, azaleas (both members of the genus *Rhododendron*) or mountain laurel (*Kalmia latifolia*), flowers whose nectars all contain chemicals, called grayanotoxins, that are psychoactive and toxic to humans but not to bees. Their effects are short lived, and symptoms include nausea, vomiting, sweating, and dizziness. Abdulkadir Gunduz and colleagues in Turkey report that "mad" honey is used locally in folk medicines as an alternative treatment for a variety of medical disorders such as gastrointestinal pain or hypertension; these claims have not been substantiated through appropriate medical testing, however.

In New Zealand, toxic honey can be found from a different source. Bees gather honeydew, a sweet secretion, from vine hopper insects, *Scolypopa australis,* that have fed on the toxic tutu bushes, *Coriaria arborea.* Symptoms of *tutin* poisoning in humans are vomiting, delirium, giddiness, stupor, and violent convulsions. Since December 2001, New Zealand beekeepers have been required to closely monitor the area within three kilometers of their hives where their bees might forage in order to prevent exposure to the toxin.

There is a Brazilian plant, *Serjania lethalis,* which produces a honey so poisonous that it has been reported to be used by native hunters for tipping their arrows and killing fish. Flowers in the Sumac genus *Rhus* make nectar that produces dark red honey (this includes *Rhus vernix,* poison sumac; and *Rhus toxicodendron,* poison ivy), but this honey is not harmful to people.

Green or unripe honey from a few plants can cause an allergic reaction in some people, and in rare cases, honey results in an allergic reaction due to contamination with pollen allergens. Honey should be considered in any patient with a food allergy that cannot be identified, because if honey is an ingredient, the patient may be having a reaction to pollen allergens in the honey. Max Deinzer and colleagues investigated alkaloids that affect the liver (hepatotoxic) that are found in the plant tansy ragwort, *Senecio jacobaea L.,* and in honey produced from its nectar. This plant is native to Europe but has widely invaded pasture lands in both North America and Australia. These alkaloids have the potential to cause cancer, mutations, and birth defects in bees, and the researchers caution that they may pose health hazards to the human consumer. Most people can consume honey without incident, and all of these ill effects are quite rare. However, honey should not be given to children under the age of one because infants may be susceptible to botulism, an illness caused by *Clostridium botulinum,* a toxin-producing bacteria that is rarely found in honey.

Mayan Beekeeping

Archeological and historical evidence indicates that the tradition of keeping bees and consuming honey and products derived from the fermentation of honey predates the arrival of *Apis mellifera* in the New World. According to Helen Ransome, when the conquering Spaniards reached Mexico and other areas in Central and South America, stingless beekeeping, or melipoculture, was already an established industry in many communities.

Prior to the European invasion of Central America, the Mayan people had a deep connection to many animals in their environment, including insects, and they often immortalized important animals into gods. They honored a "bee god" known as Ah Mucan (also written as Mucen or Muzen) Cab. The Mayans dedicated festivals to this deity to celebrate honey and mead production and used these occasions for trade and various religious ceremonies. The god is represented in carvings and art with wings expanded, as if preparing for landing or taking off. The favored species was called Xunan-Cab, which translates roughly to "royal lady." Like the modern use of the stingless Mayan bee, *Melipona beechii,* for honey production, the Mayans raised bees in special hives made out of tree branches or other containers such as logs, gourds, or clay pots. There is also evidence that they used ceremonial pottery vases to carry honey and mead, and these containers were often inscribed with hieroglyphic stories that explained how the bee god helped the local community.

Fig. 22. A pendant, carved from mother-of-pearl, that embodies the relationship between man and bees within the ancient Mayan culture. Note the bee-like abdomen connected to parts of the human body. *(Photograph K6169 © Justin Kerr, 1992.)*

Question 9: What is mead?

Answer: Mead is a fermented alcoholic beverage made from honey and water. Eva Crane writes that this alcoholic beverage was probably produced thousands of years before the creation of beers and ales, and many drinks produced from fermented honey and other ingredients have been important in multiple cultures. Mead is sometimes called honey wine; although, because it is not made from grapes, it can't properly be called wine. When mead is made with the addition of flavorings such as ginger, cloves, cinnamon, or mace, the drink is called metheglin. Bracket, also called bragget or braggot, is a type of beer brewed with more than 30 percent honey as a source of sugar, equivalent to mead brewed with malt. It was first produced as a byproduct of beekeeping in areas where grapes could not be grown, and, not unsurprisingly, it is rather sweet. Mead was mentioned in sacred texts as early as 2000 to 1100 B.C.E., and in ancient Greece mead was said to have been the preferred drink. Aristotle (384 to 322 B.C.E.) discussed mead in his *Meterologica,* and around 400 B.C.E. Plato recorded the behavior of a friend drinking nectar in the Garden of Zeus, when wine was not yet known. Hilda Ransome describes the role of mead and other bee products in multiple cultures, including Germanic myths, Welsh and Irish poems, and Mayan rituals.

EIGHT

Bees on
the Move

Question 1: Do bees ever move out of their hive?

Answer: Bees permanently move out of their hive only under two circumstances: one is called *absconding* and the other is called *swarming* (see questions and answers below.) If environmental conditions become too stressful for the bees in the colony, they can decide to stop their normal activities and abscond. This means closing up the honey shop and moving to another location, as opposed to swarming, in which the colony divides but the old nest continues to function.

Bees may abscond because the food resources in the habitat may be inadequate, for example, or the colony may become unmanageably hot due to extreme weather conditions. They do not simply leave, however, because the workers will not abandon their baby sisters—the larval and pupal brood that cannot yet fly—nor will they leave a large amount of food in the storage areas of the honeycomb. Absconding is a process during which the bees stop rearing new brood, cease foraging, and begin scouting for a new, more suitable nesting location. It isn't well studied, and it is a variable process, more common among Africanized bees than European bees.

Beekeepers can discourage bees from leaving the nest by creating optimal conditions as the colony grows by providing more space with additional hive components into which the colony can expand (see chapter 11, question 5: How does a beekeeper manage a hive?). For reasons that are not well understood, Africanized or "killer" bees are much more likely to move by absconding than European bees (see chapter 9, question 5: Do killer bees really exist?).

Question 2: What is swarming?

Answer: Swarming is a natural process by which a new colony is formed. When a hive becomes overcrowded, the worker bees instinctively know that it is time to swarm and to raise a new queen. Several large cells are created around fertilized eggs laid by the queen. When the larvae emerge from these eggs, the cells are flooded with royal jelly to foster the development of a queen rather than an ordinary female worker (see chapter 4, question 7: What is royal jelly and how does it produce a queen?). When the queen larvae are ready to enter the pupal stage, during which they will develop into adult queen bees, their cells are sealed with wax by the workers. At some point after the first queen

Fig. 23. Bees in a swarm cluster are very docile; a gentle touch does not disturb the swarm, provided the bees have ample food stored in their collective stomachs. (*Photo by Corey J. Flynn.*)

Fig. 24. A springtime swarm alights on a tree outside Marts Hall on the campus of Bucknell University. The bees are clustered around their queen. Beekeepers can collect swarms if they are located in accessible locations. (*Photo by Corey J. Flynn.*)

cell has been sealed, the old queen leaves the hive in order to avoid being killed by the new queen when she emerges. The departing queen is guided by a group of as many as ten or twenty thousand worker bees in a primary swarm. If more than one new queen emerges in the old colony and the first to emerge does not kill the others, there may be subsequent smaller "after" swarms, each led by a new queen.

Contrary to the popular belief that a swarm refers to a marauding pack of angry bees, when honey bees swarm their bellies are full of honey and they are in a gentle mood. They are prepared to stay out in the open for a day or more, and some of the bees begin producing large quantities of wax scales from glands in the abdomen in preparation for building combs in the new hive. The entire group lands temporarily in an exposed spot on the limb of a tree or on the side of a building, and they wait while some of the bees serve as scouts. The scouts find a suitable spot for the new colony and then return to direct the swarm to this new location. When the swarm arrives at the new site, they begin to build new brood combs within hours with the wax they have been secreting (see chapter 6, question 9: How do bees make beeswax?).

Question 3: How can you tell when bees are about to swarm?

Answer: A casual observer watching the outside of a honey bee nest would probably not notice anything different during the preparations for swarming, but a beekeeper examining the inside of the hive would have a different impression. The first thing you would notice when you open the top of the colony is that the bees are "boiling," overflowing out of the top of the hive. Next, while examining the honeycomb, you would see the

Fig. 25. Close-up photo of bees in a swarm; the bees are layered on top of one another in a large cluster. Bees communicate through odor and movement while in the hive and while in a swarm. *(Photo by Corey J. Flynn.)*

beginnings of the special cells where queens are reared, called "queen cups," that form the base of queen cells. They are larger than normal cells and are provisioned with royal jelly in anticipation of the hungry larval queen (see chapter 4, question 7: What is royal jelly and how does it produce a queen?). The original queen will only leave the hive (with a subset of the workers) after a replacement queen begins to grow.

When a colony swarms, an unusually loud buzzing noise can be heard, louder than the normal activity of the forager bees coming and going, and then lots of bees will begin to run outside and jump into flight. It only takes a few minutes for thousands of the insects to organize into a cloud and fly away. Watching a swarm depart from a beehive is truly a spectacular sight (see also chapter 3, question 8: What is piping behavior?).

Question 4: How does the swarm locate its new home?

Answer: While the swarm waits in a mass, hanging in an exposed location, certain worker bees that serve as scouts fly out of the swarm and search the surrounding area for suitable places to relocate the colony. The scout bees return to where the swarm is waiting, and they "report" on the places they have found, using the waggle dance (see chapter 3, question 7: What is the waggle dance?), and somehow a spot is selected. They prefer certain characteristics for a new cavity, including ample volume, and a dry space high off the ground. A consensus on the choice of a new location is reached by the scouts using a still-to-be-understood process (see chapter 3, question 6: How do bees communicate?).

Traditionally, the explanation of how the swarm finds the new location is via the dance and via olfactory cues given by scout bees. Scout bees post themselves at the entrance to the new location, and they elevate their abdomen and point it outward to expose pheromone-producing glands called Nasanov glands. The scout bees fan their wings to send out an odor trail, and it was thought that the bees in the swarm would follow the pheromone to the new site. But in 2006, Madeleine Beekman and colleagues at Cornell University reported on an experiment where they sealed the odor-releasing glands of the bees they were observing in order to see if preventing them from releasing their pheromones would disrupt the swarm's relocation. They found that sealing the glands did not interfere with the ability of the scouts to successfully direct the swarm, and they discovered that the bees were guided to the new location by "streaker" scout bees that fly very fast (up to 3.3 feet per second) above the moving swarm. Bees have three simple light-detecting organs, called ocelli, that are located on top of their head, and these organs may play a role in enabling bees to follow the streakers flying overhead. Bees' excellent ability to see fast-moving objects may also play a role in this process (see chapter 2, question 9: What do bees see?).

Question 5: What is supercedure?

Answer: Supercedure occurs when the hive replaces an aging queen. When an older queen begins to lay fewer eggs, the bees set out to replace her by rearing a queen from any fertilized eggs they can find in the brood cells. Based on the location of the queen cells, a beekeeper can determine the difference between this emergency queen-rearing during the process of supercedure and the queen-rearing in preparation for swarming. In preparation for swarming, bees rear queens on the bottom of the brood combs, but during supercedure queen cells are randomly dispersed. Some beekeepers will immediately replace the queen when they see this evidence of supercedure, because they believe that the resulting queen will be substandard due to the emergency nature of the process.

Question 6: Do bees migrate?

Answer: Most bees don't migrate, but species of honey bees that are native to Southeast Asia migrate long distances to avoid the stressful environmental conditions associated with the monsoon season. The giant honey bee, *Apis dorsata* (a sister species

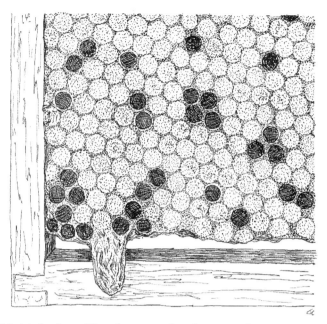

Fig. 26. Made of wax, like other types of comb, queen cells are elongated growth chambers that house the growing queens (*lower left*). Queen cells on the bottom of comb indicate swarming and in the middle of comb indicate emergency queen rearing. (*Drawing by John F. Cullum.*)

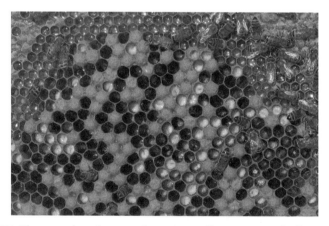

Fig. 27. The spotty brood pattern (some open cells, some capped cells containing pupae, some larvae) on this comb indicates that the queen is laying eggs inconsistently—a sign of queen aging. An alert beekeeper may decide to replace the queen to keep the colony productive. (*Photo by Debra Cook-Balducci.*)

to the western or European honey bee *Apis mellifera*), is native to Thailand and India; these bees regularly abandon their nests and move into areas that have better food resources during the time of year when their normal food sources disappear, and they come back when the dry weather returns. *A. dorsata* colonies resemble the vertical combs of *A. mellifera,* but they differ in that they do not nest inside a cavity. Instead, they build exposed beeswax combs that are at risk for being damaged or destroyed by the rains.

Many bees involuntarily migrate when roving beekeepers in the United States load up a tractor-trailer filled with honey bee colonies and transport them across the country to be temporarily located near flowering crops that require insect pollination in order to develop fruit (see chapter 6, question 5: How do farmers make sure there are enough bees to pollinate their crops?). Douglas Whynott has written a fascinating account of these bee "cowboys" in his book entitled *Following the Bloom: Across America with the Migratory Beekeepers.* Moving hundreds of colonies across the country—from Florida (for oranges), to South Carolina (for melons), to New York (for apples), to Maine (for blueberries), to California (for almonds)—these migrating pollinators have become an industry that supports commercial agriculture.

Question 7: How far do bees fly?

Answer: Scout bees regularly look for food around their hives, and they typically travel within a four- to five-mile radius. Most foragers concentrate on food sources that are within about two miles from their nest, depending on the availability of local flowers, but when hives are located far from food sources, bees can fly longer distances. In a classic series of experiments to study how far bees can fly, honey bees are trained to feed from artificial flowers laced with a sugar solution (see figure 26). When the feeders are gradually moved away from the hive with feeding bees on them, observations by Karl von Frisch and his many students indicate that bees can travel up to twelve miles from the nest to obtain food.

Fig. 28. Honey bees can be trained to visit an artificial flower filled with scented sugar syrup. This technique can be used to study the waggle dance or orientation behavior in an observation hive. *(Photo by Elizabeth Capaldi Evans.)*

Question 8: How high do bees fly?

Answer: The real answer to this question is not so much limited by the bees' flight ability, but rather by their reason for flying high. Bees can and do fly to the height of the tallest trees in order to reach flowers; in rainforests, there are trees that are two hundred feet tall, which would not be a problem for hungry bees. Bees can also be seen visiting flowers on window boxes on tall apartment buildings without any sign of physiological stress. The real limit to bee flight is temperature, which declines at high altitudes, and they cannot fly when temperatures are below about 45 degrees Fahrenheit (7 degrees Celsius).

Question 9: How do bees locate nectar-rich flowers?

Answer: Bees primarily use their keen visual abilities to find profitable flowers that advertise their nectar or pollen rewards with bright or showy flowers. Flowers that attract bees typically

The Great Pollinator Research Project in New York City

New York City has a surprisingly large number of bee species living in the parks, gardens, and neighborhoods of its five boroughs. Sixty species have been counted in Central Park, for example, and a community garden in East Harlem boasted 28 species at last count. Bees and beehives are also found on rooftops, terraces, and in backyards on some of the greener city streets. There are even specialists affiliated with the police department who are dispatched to retrieve honey bee swarms when people phone in to report them clinging to traffic signals or street lights. Kevin Matteson of Fordham University, along with John Ascher of the American Museum of Natural History and Gail Langellotto of Oregon State University, studied nineteen of the over seven hundred community gardens in the city for a period that included four growing seasons. They identified 225 species of bees in New York City, 88 species in Manhattan alone.

In 2007, prompted by recent declines in the populations of European honey bees and native bumblebees, the American Museum of Natural History's Center for Biodiversity and Conservation and the New York City Department of Parks and Recreation's Greenbelt Native Plant Center decided to work together to gather more information about New York City's bee populations with a long-term goal of increasing bee habitat and diversity in the city. In collaboration with the Great Sunflower Project, they launched New York City Bee Watchers—a citizen science project to recruit volunteers from the five boroughs to help gather data. According to Elizabeth Johnson, one of the leaders of the project, the goals of the project are to "identify which areas of New York City have good pollinator service (as determined by how quickly bees show up to pollinate flowers at various locations throughout the city), to increase understanding of bee distribution, to raise public awareness of native bees, and to improve park management practices to benefit native bees." The project is

(continued)

yielding valuable data that will contribute to bee conservation management strategies.

There are about 150 volunteers who collect data twice a month about bee activity on certain flowers in New York City as part of this project. Each volunteer planted his or her seven plants somewhere in a park or garden in one of New York City's five boroughs. To simplify identification for novice bee watchers, the study asks participants to divide their bees into one of four categories: bumblebees, honey bees, carpenter bees, and green metallic bees.

Janet David is a long-time Manhattan resident who joined the project as a volunteer bee watcher as an extension of her volunteer activities at the American Museum of Natural History. Before participating in this study, Janet admits she had no idea of the variety and quantity of bees that can be found in New York City. Her study area consists of six flowering plants native to the city that she planted in May in the southern end of Central Park in Manhattan: common milkweed, woodland sunflower, wild bergamot, rough-leaved goldenrod, slender-leaved mountain mint, and smooth aster.

To do her observation, Janet takes along a data sheet, a watch, a set of photos of the bees for identification, and her camera. The camera is helpful when the bee identification is difficult because, as Janet noted, "Bees are fast!" Observations are done on two weekends a month when the weather is sunny and calm, preferably from 10 to 12 a.m., but they can be done until 3 p.m. Following the protocol, Janet observes her area for thirty minutes or until five bees have landed on her study flowers—she says sometimes five bees land in less than five minutes.

When doing an observation, Janet records the exact location of her study plants so that the data can be charted with a GPS navigation system. She notes the date and time she starts the observation, the time each bee lands on a study flower,

The Great Pollinator Research Project in New York City

the name of the flower she is watching, the types of bees that land on her flowers, the air temperature, and an estimate of the number of flowers nearby. When possible, she submits photos of the plants and the bees.

As a result of participating in this research, Janet feels she is certainly more observant about different kinds of bees— and less afraid of them. One of the first things the volunteers learned is that bees rarely sting unless their nests are disturbed. Janet is aware that she looks at and tastes honey in a different way; she even recently noticed that Haagen Dazs Ice Cream has a new honey-flavored ice cream. So, as Janet put it, "That's the buzz about bees in New York City."

To volunteer or learn more, go to www.nycbeewatchers.org.

have yellow, blue, or purple flowers, often with radiating colors that emerge from a central point (see color plate C). Bees can see flower colors as they fly over the landscape, and floral odors are secondary cues that can help bees zero in on their targets. Because floral scents are not detectable over long distances, odors are probably only used to back up the visual information.

Question 10: How do foraging bees find their way home?

Answer: A scout bee will leave the nest without a definite destination. She will embark on a search for food resources, and as she moves she is actually noticing cues in the environment that will guide her flight home. Bees can gather directional information from celestial cues, such as the position of the sun and the sun-linked patterns of polarization that are present in the sky (see chapter 3, question 13: How do bees sense and use polarized light?). Interestingly, young adult bees must learn the sky-light compass when they first begin to fly outside the nest. This was shown in experiments by Jeff Dickinson and Fred Dyer, which demonstrated that bees are not born with the ability to use this information. The second type of information, place or location, must also be learned. Bees recognize visual landmarks in the environment, such as tree lines, buildings, landscape features like hills or ridges, and use those images to build a map of their world.

In short, bees have the ability to "dead reckon" after a scouting trip. They may take an outward path that meanders around the landscape, but when they want to head home, they can simply integrate their map and compass information and fly directly home. Without experience, or without these two sources of information, a bee cannot directly find her way home, but she may be able to do so after flying in a random search pattern.

Question 11: What happens to flying bees in bad weather?

Answer: Bees have special hairs that act like sensors on their bodies to adjust their flight path in relation to wind speed and direction, enabling them to maintain a straight course of flight. In extremely hard wind, bees will take shelter in vegetation until the winds have slowed down.

Bees can only fly in very light rain. During heavy rain, the large droplets of water can actually knock bees down. Another problem that accompanies rain is low air temperature. When bees are wet, their ability to generate metabolic heat in order to stay warm enough to fly becomes very taxed. Bumblebees, which have larger bodies than honey bees, can fly at lower temperatures and also are better able to tolerate some rain. In short, honey bees don't like rain, and they usually stay at home when it rains rather than look for food.

Question 12: What is playflight behavior?

Answer: If you were to visit a honey bee hive on a warm, sunny afternoon, you might see a large cloud of bees hovering just in front of the beehive in a way that differs from the normal, busy traffic of the foragers. Austrian scientist Karl von Frisch and others studying bee behavior first called this behavior *vorspiel* (playing about). When further examined, this behavior, now called playflight behavior or orientation flight behavior, occurs when the young adult bees take their first flights outside of the nest. This activity has a serious purpose and has nothing to do with play.

As honey bees age, their behavior changes in a regular and predictable fashion, and the oldest bees in the colony have the risky job of venturing into the outside world (see chapter 1, question 9: What is the role of the workers?). But first they need to learn about their environment, so they can efficiently scout and forage without getting lost. Bees must integrate a lot of information in their middle age involving the location of their hive entrance, the sky-light compass, and how to find and handle flowers efficiently. Playflight behavior occurs when they begin this process by taking orientation or reconnaissance flights outside of the nest, and they return from these flights without food, water, or any other resource except information. The cloud of bees seen during a playflight occurs because lots of young bees take these flights at one time. Without playflight behavior, bees cannot learn to navigate. What triggers the behavior is unknown, but we do know that it typically happens between 1 p.m. and 3 p.m. on warm, sunny days. Interestingly, beehives kept indoors for long periods of time in experimental flight rooms with an artificial light-dark cycle still exhibit these bursts of activity, even though the bees presumably cannot detect the environmental cues for the specific time of day.

NINE

Bee Stings and Other Defenses

Question 1: Do all bees sting?

Answer: Not all bees can sting. The bee's sting is a modification of the *ovipositor,* the female egg-laying organ, and so no males of any bee species sting. Most people are surprised to know that the stinger is kept inside the bee's body until it is used. Unless you see a bee trying to sting you, you will not see the stinger as a bee flies by or feeds from a flower. There is a group of social bees in the tropics that are not capable of stinging. They either lack stingers or have reduced sting structures without the necessary muscles to extend them as weapons. In this stingless bee family, females can defend themselves from harmful predators using other strategies (see chapter 9, question 7: How do stingless bees defend themselves?).

Female worker bees are generally quite peaceful, and they are only inclined to sting when an intruder threatens the colony or when they are alarmed by unfamiliar odors or high-contrast patterns that are easiest for them to see. The queen bee also has a stinger, but she uses it to lay eggs and only stings other queens in order to kill them and prevent them from emerging and threatening her dominance (see chapter 4, question 8: How is the queen bee chosen?).

Question 2: What does it feel like to be stung by a bee?

Answer: Though the amount of venom in a honey bee sting is small, it can cause a great deal of discomfort and occasional harm. One author describes a bee sting as similar to a car door slamming on your fingers. Others describe it as feeling like touching a hot match. To make matters worse, the stinging bee emits an alarm pheromone that calls for reinforcements, increasing the potential for more toxins to be injected by the bees that respond to her signal.

The face and ears are most vulnerable to bee stings, probably because these are the areas where bee predators have the thinnest hair. Bees may also cue on exhaled carbon dioxide to focus their attacks in vulnerable areas. Beekeepers almost always wear a hat and veil, even if they don't wear other protective clothing. Some beekeepers who have been stung many times build up a tolerance and become effectively immune to the venom.

Question 3: How does a bee sting?

Answer: The bee's sting is normally retracted inside her abdomen, which is the third or end section of the bee's body. When she is alarmed, the sting drops and locks into place like the landing gear on an airplane, and muscles in the abdomen thrust the stinger into its target. When the victim is another insect, the stinger can be used repeatedly, but if she stings a fleshy target, the barbed sting breaks away and is typically left embedded in the victim's flesh. When the sting breaks off, the venom sac protruding from the end of the sting is often still visibly pumping venom even though it has been torn from the bee's body. A bee that has lost its sting will die soon after.

Question 4: Why do bees sting?

Answer: It is impossible to know if bees feel anger, but their behavior can be quite aggressive if they sense signs of disturbance or imminent danger to the stability of the nest, and they

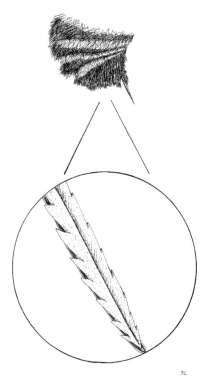

Fig. 29. Honey bee stingers are normally kept inside the abdomen; a close-up image reveals the serrated edges of these defensive weapons. *(Drawing by John F. Cullum.)*

seem to be able to moderate their responses depending on the nature of the risk they perceive. The risk is highest at the nest, rather than on flowers in fields, which is why most bee stings occur near the nest. Most bees will not sting without some trigger because the consequences can be costly. Depending on the target, stinging may cause the bee's stinger to break off, which results in the bee's death in short order.

Some scientists have described the triggers to many bee behaviors as being dependent on thresholds of response that can change depending upon the bee's age and experience. For example, perhaps only certain bees in the colony would sting a perceived intruder, depending on the bee's age and social role. For those that wouldn't sting, their hypothetical response threshold would be higher, and they would need to feel more threatened before they would react by stinging. The condition of the colony, the local environment, and even the weather can play a role in whether or not a bee will sting. According to Samuel Beshers and Jennifer Fewell, the response threshold idea may also help explain how the honey bee colony is organized by division of labor, so that each bee, depending on the social environment and work to be done, receives signals that either hit or miss their individual threshold level of response for that behavior.

Question 5: Do killer bees really exist?

Answer: Africanized honey bees are known popularly as "killer bees," although their venom is no more toxic than that of the common European honey bee. They are dangerous because they can be very aggressive when their colony is disturbed and sometimes thousands at a time will sting one victim, flooding the person or animal with multiple doses of venom that can reach highly toxic levels. Although many people can survive an attack like this, it can be lethal to children or physically vulnerable adults.

Killer bees are all hybrids, descendants of twenty-six Tanzanian queen bees, *Apis mellifera scutellata,* and various strains of European bees with which they have mated. The Tanzanian bees were accidentally released in 1957 from a breeding program in Brazil which was attempting to artificially select for bee traits that would produce more honey and better pollinators in tropical conditions. Prior to the European colonization of North and South America, no honey bees lived in these areas, so we know that any honey bees in Brazil prior to 1957 were of European origin. Since that time, the hybrid bees have moved north through South and Central America and, more recently, into North America.

Mark Winston of Simon Fraser University describes how beekeeping has been affected by these bees and their unique traits: "Indeed, the politics of the Africanized honey bee, and the media attention to it, have caused us to lose sight of the unprecedented success story of an introduced species that is elegantly preadapted to its new environment. The bee is so well suited to tropical life that we have not been able to devise a way to stop or even slow its spread. We marvel at its success in the wild, even as we struggle to blunt its impact on beekeeping and the public." Africanized bees have established themselves in an increasingly wide area of the United States, and at their peak rate of expansion they spread north at a rate of almost a mile or about two kilometers a day.

By 2002, these aggressive bees had been seen to the south in Argentina and to the north as far as Trinidad in the West Indies, Mexico, Texas, Arizona, New Mexico, Florida, and southern California. In June 2005, they were found in southwest Arkansas, and in 2007 they were reported in the New Orleans area. They are said to have caused eleven deaths in Texas in the fifteen years that they have been in the area. They occasionally are seen in northern ports, probably after being transported by ships that move through the Panama Canal. So far, no way has been found to stop their expansion, but regular population monitoring and swarm trapping is conducted by both local and federal government agencies. Africanized bees are not adapted to cold temperatures, so their continued overwintering survival and expansion into northern regions of the United States may be limited.

Question 6: Does a bee die after it has stung somebody?

Answer: If a honey bee stings a person, its stinger usually breaks off in the person's body and the bee usually dies within a few minutes. The ancestors of bees were parasitic wasps, and they needed an ovipositor (their egg-laying organ) that could pierce the hard outer exoskeleton of an insect in order to lay their eggs inside its body, using it as a host for the developing eggs. Stingers and their associated poison glands evolved to protect the colony against invading insects, especially bees from different hives. Interestingly, most wasp and bee stingers are straight, like a sewing needle, but the stinger of a honey bee is barbed. The barbed stinger can penetrate another insect's *exoskeleton* and retract safely, leaving the bee intact and able to sting again; but it breaks off in soft flesh, so a honey bee worker can only sting a person once, whereas other types of bees and wasps can sting people multiple times. Queen honey bees can sting, but they very rarely use their stinger for defense, probably because it could risk damaging their ovipositor, which is central to their role in the colony.

Question 7: How do stingless bees defend themselves?

Answer: Meliponid or stingless bees have vestigial or atrophied stingers and are not capable of stinging (see chapter 1, question 3: How many species of bees exist?). Although most species of stingless bees are generally mild-mannered, a few species will defend themselves by biting fiercely when they are threatened, and Dylan Voeller and James Nieh have filmed *Trigona spinipes* and *Melipona rufiventris* fighting viciously over food. David Roubik, Brian Smith, and R. G. Carlson described at least two species within the *Oxytrigona* genus that secrete caustic salivary substances made up of formic acids and other defensive chemicals, making their bite extremely uncomfortable. The stingless bee *Trigona fulviventris* marks potential predators with a chemical secretion that elicits additional bees to react defensively by buzzing, biting, and hair pulling.

Another species enters the eyes, ears, and nose of the threatening animal or person and then buzzes its wings loudly; this strategy is an effective way to make a predator run away from the bee nest. Other species will attack a potential nest intruder with sticky nest substances, like resins or honey. Being covered in gooey materials discourages further nest intrusions.

Alexandros Papachristoforou studied Cyprian honey bees *Apis mellifera cypria* that have an interesting way of defending themselves against the local Oriental hornets *Vespa orientalis*. Hornets, like all insects, breathe through *spiracles,* which are holes in their exoskeleton. They contract their abdominal muscles to exhale and relax the muscles to inhale, and these muscle

Stingless Bees

While beekeeping for honey and wax production mainly relies on the behavior of the European or Western honey bee *Apis mellifera,* other social bees are also raised and kept in managed colonies for the production of honey, wax, and pollen. Stingless bees in the family Meliponidae have long played a part in providing people in Central America with renewable hive products as well as being a regular source of local pollinators.

Like honey bees, stingless bees are highly social bees that nest in cavities, but they do not sting. They also exhibit age-polytheism, which is the predictable change of tasks that occurs with aging in some social insects; and they use a symbolic form of communication to recruit nest mates to profitable food sources, albeit one that differs from the waggle dance of the honey bee.

Another way that stingless bees differ from honey bees is the way they feed their brood. Honey bees continually bring food to their young, but stingless bees "mass provision" their young, collecting pollen and placing it in brood cells along with glandular secretions and nectar or honey. The queen lays an egg on this mixture of food, and then workers enclose the newly laid egg within the cell. They will not meet their new sibling again until it emerges into the colony as an adult. One advantage of this style of feeding offspring is that there is a reduction of disease transmission within the colony because there is less communication between the generations.

Another important difference between honey bees and stingless bees is in the structure of their nests. Stingless bee nests have a physical separation between the brood area and the food storage area. The brood cells look more like little jelly beans arranged in sheets, layers, or clusters, while the food cells resemble small pots that can be as large as a kidney bean. Many species of stingless bees have nests with food areas that can be removed from the colony without disrupting the brood, but the food cells cannot be replaced, as is the case with honey bees. Stingless bee nests can supply people with

Stingless Bees

wax and honey, provided attention is given to the timing of nest disruption and the prevention of attack from ants or nest parasites. With some species, pots of pollen are removed along with the pots of honey, which adds to the flavor of the honey.

Honey from stingless bees is a valuable commodity in many local communities in Latin America, where it is believed to be a healthy elixir. Stingless bee honey is lower in sugar content and is usually less viscous than the honey from *Apis mellifera,* but many people prefer its taste. In Panama, some small stingless bees, *Trigona angustula,* are known as *angelitas* because they are thought to be guardian angels of the home. These bees are kept both by individuals and, in some communities, by specialist beekeepers. The colonies are typically suspended under the eves of buildings. One species of particular interest is *Melipona beechii;* in Honduras these bees are known as *estrella blanca,* or "white star," bees because of the distinctive, star-like nest entrance these bees construct. Because they close their colonies with new wax every evening, the entrance becomes a "white star" each day (see color plate F).

Unfortunately, stingless bee culture is on the decline across many areas of Central America. David Roubik, a scientist working at the Smithsonian Tropical Research Institute in Panama who is known around the world as the "Bee Man," reported that the loss of these cultured bees in areas of the Yucatan Peninsula could have a dramatic impact on the pollination ecology of the local flora, as these native bees often work as pollinators for plants not visited by honey bees.

Melipoculture (raising stingless bees) is ripe for local development in many places since keeping these bees is less expensive than keeping honey bees and does not typically require the protective beekeeping equipment needed for apiculture. Ester Slaa, a tropical bee researcher from the University of Leeds, and her coauthors from Brazil, Costa Rica, and the Netherlands, describe stingless bees as strong candidates for

(continued)

Stingless Bees, *continued*

use as commercial pollinators and report that at least eleven species of stingless bees forage effectively on crops grown in greenhouses. Tim Heard, in a review of these bees as pollinators, reports that stingless bees pollinate coffee plants, tomatoes, peppers, cucumbers, mangos, avocados, sweet peppers, and others. Slaa and her colleagues advocate for more integration between agricultural crops, habitat conservation, and the promotion of melipoculture.

movements open and close plates in the exoskeleton that protect the holes. The researchers found that bees cluster around the hornet to defend against it, and they actually suffocate the hornet by making it impossible for it to open its spiracles to take in air. This form of asphyxiation has not been documented as a defense against other invaders, but it is a strategy that could work against many other insects.

Japanese honey bees, *Apis cerana japonica,* guard against their local, predatory hornets, *Vespa simillima xanthoptera,* in a different way. Both the bees and the hornets are accustomed to a relatively cool climate, and Masato Ono and colleagues found that when bees are threatened by a hornet, a huge group of bees *thermoballs* it, surrounding the predatory hornet in a cluster and vibrating their muscles until they heat the hornet to a temperature that kills it (113 degrees Fahrenheit, 45 degrees Celsius). This form of thermal strategy seems to be a rare type of colony defense, and it is not commonly seen against other intruders.

Question 8: Is being stung by a bee dangerous?

Answer: Although bee stings can be painful, they only rarely cause serious complications. The discomfort and localized swelling caused by a normal reaction to a bee sting can last for several days but is not a cause for alarm. Taking antihistamines can ease the discomfort of a sting as can the application of an ice pack to the sting site. A beekeeper who has been stung many times can build up a tolerance and will not swell in response to a sting: people may become effectively immune to the venom, but there is a range of possible reactions.

There are fifty to one hundred deaths in the United States each year from insect stings, about half of which come from honey bees. In highly allergic individuals, bee stings can result in anaphylaxis, which causes the throat to swell shut and the blood pressure to drop, which can be followed by shock, unconsciousness, and even death if left untreated. This type of anaphylactic response to a bee sting is rare, however, and can be treated via professional medical intervention. People who think they are having an extreme allergic reaction should seek immediate medical help and discuss desensitization procedures with an allergist.

Africanized bees (also called killer bees) are very aggressive and attack in large groups when they are threatened, which can result in a victim being stung repeatedly, in some cases thousands of times (see this chapter, question 5: Do killer bees really exist?). The amount of venom injected in such an attack can be so large that it can be lethal. The amount of venom in a single honey bee sting, by comparison, is tiny.

Question 9: What is bee venom?

Answer: Venom is a complex mixture of chemicals, including a toxic protein called *melittin,* which bursts blood vessels and damages tissues. Emollient enzymes act like water on a dry sponge, maximizing the toxins' spread into the tissues. Neurotransmitters are stimulated in the brain that accentuate the fear and excitement felt by the victim, and the venom stimulates the victim's body to release histamines that produce itching, redness, and swelling as a side effect of defending itself against the toxin. Bee venom is available in various forms and with different degrees of purity (it can contain traces of pollen, honey, dust, feces, or nectar), and it can be processed and freeze dried.

There are unproven uses for bee venom, such as to treat cancer, multiple sclerosis, chronic pain, joint diseases, and skin diseases. In many countries, bee venom is a component of prescription and non-prescription creams, liniments, ointments and salves, and injectable compounds. Some beekeepers claim that a bee sting on a painful spot provides excellent pain relief, and some people use bee venom to treat arthritis. Some veterinarians use bee venom injections to treat horses and dogs with arthritis.

Question 10: Does collecting venom kill the bees?

Answer: During the 1950s and '60s, bee venom was collected using a wooden or plastic collection frame with an electrified wire grid placed at the entrance of a hive. Under the wires was a glass sheet that was covered with plastic or rubber, and the bees came in contact with the wire and received an electric shock that would cause the bees to sting the rubber sheet, paralyzing their muscles and usually electrocuting them. If that didn't kill them, when they stung the surface of the collector sheet their stinger would generally break off, resulting in death. Their venom was deposited between the glass and the rubber or plastic, where it was allowed to dry, and then it was scraped off and collected.

Newer collection methods claim to be safe and relatively harmless. In 2005 the first microprocessor-controlled bee-venom collector device went on the market, capable of collecting venom from up to one hundred hives at a time. The newer devices use the same principle as the older frames, but their circuitry allows them to administer very low levels of voltage, just at the threshold that stimulates the bees to sting but is not enough to kill them. Also, the newer devices have replaced the rubber collection sheet with a high-tech diaphragm that does not kill the bees by causing the stinger to break off. The manufacturer reports that during thirty to sixty minutes of collecting using the latest device, fewer than five bees will be killed, not a significant loss to a thriving colony.

Question 11: How can you avoid being stung by a bee?

Answer: The best way not to be stung by a bee is to stay away from bee colonies, because bees are very reluctant to sting unless their nest is threatened or disturbed. For the most part, it is easy to avoid honey bee nests because they tend to live in managed colonies, which are typically large, white boxes. Occasionally, people will be surprised to find themselves near a bumblebee nest in the ground.

If a bee is nearby, the best strategy to avoid being stung is to ignore it—most bees will simply fly by, as people do not usually have anything of interest to them and bees are not usually in an aggressive state when foraging away from the hive. Waving your arms around can touch or threaten the bees, and accidental stings can result. Another anti-sting strategy is not to wear strong perfume or cologne and to wear light-colored clothing. Bees will sometimes investigate high-contrast patterns, especially if they are accompanied by distinctive or sweet smells.

Picnic tables are often the sites where people encounter what they think are bees, but in reality, the stinging insects that visit picnics are usually wasps known as yellow jackets. Bees, as strict vegetarians, do not find much to eat at picnic tables, and they do not like cans of soda pop as much as wasps do!

Question 12: Are there any natural remedies for bee stings?

Answer: Most so-called natural remedies have not been scientifically assessed for their effectiveness against bee stings. That said, anything that reduces swelling, like the application of an ice pack, can ease the discomfort of a bee sting. A poultice of water and baking soda or even meat tenderizer may also alleviate the itch of a bee sting. Other remedies that are sometimes mentioned include putting a slice of onion or potato on the site of the sting or washing the area with cider vinegar.

TEN

Dangers to Bees

Question 1: What dangers threaten bees in the environment?

Answer: Poor nutrition, disease, parasitic mites (see this chapter, question 3: What parasites and insects prey on bees?), pesticides, and pollution are some of the threats that stress colonies and cause them to fail. Honey bees are totally dependent on the weather for creating their food supply, and malnutrition is common when a lack of rain or extreme temperatures interfere with the normal bloom cycle of plants that are their nectar and pollen sources. A rainy period keeps the bees inside the colony, forcing them to use up food that had been stored for the winter, and if the weather has been poor, plants may not be robust and the pollen may not contain the usual proteins, vitamins, and other substances required by the bees. If bees are in poor health, they are more susceptible to disease, including about twenty known viruses to which bees are vulnerable (see this chapter, question 2: How do bees survive harsh weather?).

Insecticides are used as a seed treatment and in spray applications on plants. They become distributed throughout the tissues of the plants and can cause a toxic reaction when bees consume the nectar and pollen. Pollution also threatens habitat, as do housing developments and other large ground-clearing projects like airports, golf courses, and intensive agricultural projects that completely remove habitat.

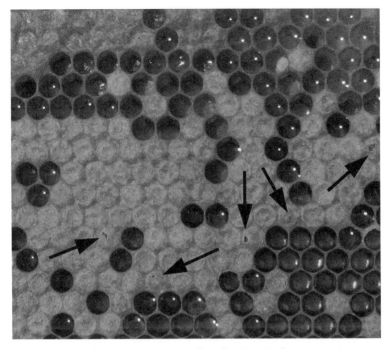

Fig. 30. The black arrows point to small perforations in the wax cappings over brood; these are signs of stress in an otherwise healthy colony. Some beekeepers believe that these imperfections signal future trouble within the colony, despite the absence of any current disease. *(Photo by Debra Cook-Balducci.)*

Question 2: How do bees survive harsh weather?

Answer: Rain provides a hazard for bees, including the danger of being knocked out of the sky by a big raindrop. When it rains, the bees stay in the colony and survive on stored food. An extended rainy period can deplete supplies stored for the winter, endangering the survival of the colony. If foragers are caught away from their colony by a sudden rainstorm or cold snap, they sometimes take shelter under flowers or vegetation until the weather conditions improve enough for them to head homeward.

In the warm weather, bees are very active, but in winter they become sluggish and their metabolism slows. So-called warm-blooded animals regulate their metabolism and maintain a relatively constant body temperature regardless of the temperature in the environment, and although cold-blooded creatures like bees and other insects are hot when their environment is hot and cold when their environment is cold, they do have some control over their body temperature through a process called thermoregulation.

Thermoregulation enables bees to adjust their body temperature by generating some heat when their environment is cool by, for example, shivering and crowding together. On cold winter days, bees keep warm by clumping together in large groups and beating their wings in order to produce heat, alternating positions on the colder perimeter of the cluster with their sisters who have warmer spots in the middle. The temperature in the center of the cluster averages 21 degrees Celsius (almost 70 degrees Fahrenheit), with a manageable range of approximately 12 to 34 degrees Celsius (54 to 94 degrees Fahrenheit). L. Fahrenholz and colleagues at the University of Berlin found that if the central temperature falls below about 15 degrees Celsius (59 degrees Fahrenheit) and the peripheral temperature is even lower, the bees are in danger.

The colony is more stable in the winter because the queen stops laying eggs and there are no fragile larvae requiring constant care and feeding. Honey bees can survive a normal winter sheltered in the hive, in a hollow tree, or in some other cavity, as long as they have enough stored honey to provide a source of energy. Most beekeepers only harvest the honey made during the spring and early summer for themselves, leaving the honey made from late summer and early fall flowering plants for the hive to consume during the cold weather. After the bees have eaten the honey in one part of the hive, they move in a cluster to another part where there is more honey. The bees tend to move from the lower honey storage areas of the hive (supers) to the upper supers during the winter. Some bees die when it gets too cold, and some species survive by migrating to warmer areas or by moving underground.

When external temperatures rise, bees increase the space between their bodies to help distribute the heat their bodies give off (metabolic heat), and they actively cool the hive in several ways. They may allow fluid droplets to evaporate from within their mouth to remove extra heat from the body, the bee's version of perspiration in mammals. When the colony is very hot, certain foragers will collect water, which they distribute in drops around the hive, and other bees will fan their wings to increase the air circulation and evaporate the water to remove some of the heat. When all else fails, the adult bees will hang as a group on the outside of the colony to totally remove their body heat from the brood area, a maneuver described by some beekeepers as a "beard." The hive would then be "bearded out," apparently wearing a beard made of bees.

The brood (the developing bees) needs to be kept at a stable temperature in order to grow normally, and during the summer season the temperature in the brood nest is maintained at 34.5 degrees Celsius (94 degrees Fahrenheit), with a range of plus or minus 1.5 degrees Celsius. Julia Jones and her colleagues, Madeline Beekman, Ryszard Maleszka, Ben Oldroyd, and Paul Helliwell, in Australia did experiments in which they transferred groups of brood cells into seven incubators that were kept at a different but constant temperatures, ranging from 31 to 37 degrees Celsius (87 to 99 degrees Fahrenheit). The brood cells were put into the incubators within one day of being capped, which indicates the beginning of the pupal phase. Seven days after the bees emerged from their brood cells, 378 bees were tested for long-term memory and 546 were tested for short-term memory.

To test the bees' memory, each bee was trained to associate a lemony scent with a reward of sucrose so that when the scent was detected, the bee would extend its proboscis in anticipation of the reward. Then they tested some of the bees after one hour and another group after twenty-four hours, to see if they extended the proboscis when they were exposed to the scent, which would indicate that the bees remembered the training experience. The study found that abnormal incubation temperatures had an effect on short-term learning and memory but that long-term learning and memory did not prove to be significantly affected by the temperature at which the pupae were reared. This suggests that there are some important neurological consequences of not maintaining the temperature within the desired range, and this could have some subtle impact on the development of optimal foraging ability.

Adult winter bees can live for several months, but when some die naturally, workers carry out their dead sisters and drop their bodies at a distance from the hive. On a warm day in the winter, bees will take cleansing flights. They do not defecate inside the hive, and indigestible material naturally found in honey and pollen accumulates in their intestines. If they cannot fly from time to time to eliminate waste from their bodies, they become ill and die. Some beekeepers remove the honey from small colonies during the winter, replacing it with high-fructose corn syrup, which is quite pure with no indigestible matter, allowing the bees to be kept for long periods without the need to void. In very cold areas in the northern United States and in Canada, some commercial beekeepers kill their bees at the end of each honey-gathering season and start the spring with a new package of bees purchased from a supplier. This strategy is not very common.

Question 3: What parasites and insects prey on bees?

Answer: Large dragonflies and hornets catch honey bees on the wing and feed on them, and many other bee predators are insects. The major insect pathogens and parasites are described below in some detail.

Varroa mites

Varroa destructor mites were introduced in the United States in 1987 from the Asian hive bee *Apis cerana,* and they spread across the country in five years, living up to their name by killing many American honey bees. They are eight-legged external parasites that can only reproduce in a honey bee colony, although they are sometimes found on other flower-feeding insects. *Varroa* mites feed on the hemolymph of bees in the larval and pupal stages. They are called *ectoparasites* because they stay on the outside of the bees as they feed, creating open wounds which make the weakened bees vulnerable to pathogens. Certain viruses can cause the pupal bees to develop deformities that include the possible absence of a leg, crumpled or vestigial wings, a shortened abdomen, or an overall reduction in size. If infested bees survive and are able to fly, their ability to forage normally does not seem to be impaired, but there may be non-lethal behavioral impacts about which we know very little. There are some chemicals

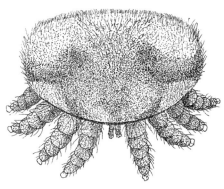

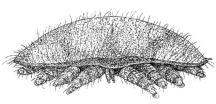

Fig. 31. These diagrams show the ectoparasite *Varroa destructor.* These mites cause physiological stress for bees and problems for beekeepers. The *top* image is a dorsal view, the *middle* is a side view, and the *bottom* illustrates mites on a honey bee pupa. (*Drawing by John F. Cullum.*)

that dissuade mite populations, but some mites have become immune to these drugs.

Tracheal mites

Tracheal mites, *Acarapis woodi,* are small, spider-like *endoparasites* that infest the breathing tubes, or trachea, of honey bees, feeding on a bee's hemolymph from inside the bee's body. Dense infestations of tracheal mites can result in colony death during the winter months because, with many mites in the trachea, the bees cannot breathe normally and aren't able to regulate the colony's temperature. Jon Harrison and his colleagues at Arizona State University studied the impact of mite infestation on the breathing of bees.

These mites are normally found on an Asian cousin of the European honey bee, and they were first identified in Mexico in 1980 and then found in Texas in 1984 and in southern Arizona in 1988. While it is unpleasant to think about it this way, tracheal mites exist like lice on people—the infection is present in low numbers, and they do not do much permanent damage to people suffering with them. Why tracheal mites jumped onto a new species is not understood, and, unfortunately, there is no clear treatment to prevent them except for keeping colonies strong and healthy.

Wax moths

There are two moth species that feed on the materials inside a beehive—both are generally called wax moths, but they are different creatures: the greater wax moth, *Galleria mellonella,* and the lesser wax moth, *Achroia grisella.* As adults, they are small, grayish-brown, and nocturnal, and they both have a keen ability to detect beeswax, in which they lay hundreds of tiny eggs. Wax moth larvae eat the larval skins that are shed when the adult bees emerge, and they also eat impurities in the wax of the bee brood combs, such as pollen and all sorts of debris carried on the thousands of bee feet that have walked across it. If a bee colony is healthy and strong, meaning it has a full complement of workers, the bees can detect and remove the moth larvae be-

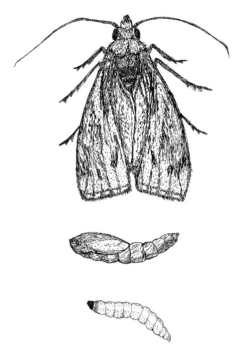

Fig. 32. A wax moth adult, pupa, and larva. These animals lay hundreds of eggs in weak or abandoned beehives. The eggs grow into larvae that damage the honeycombs. (*Drawing by John F. Cullum.*)

fore too much damage is done to the colony, but as the larvae grow, they burrow into the wax and can render the combs inhospitable to bees.

These whitish-gray larvae are certainly not a pleasant sight in a beehive, leaving trails of silk behind them as they move and dig into the wax (see color plate H). Freezing the wax honey frames after the honey has been extracted can kill wax moths eggs and larvae. Wax moths also do not like the fumes of various chemicals, such as paradichlorobenzene (PBD), which is an appropriate (and legal) preventative treatment against these pests and does not hurt the bees. PBD cannot be used in colonies that are actively storing honey because this fumigant is not safe for human exposure or consumption.

Bee lice

A bee louse is actually a tiny wingless fly, *Braula coeca,* which lives inside bee colonies. They cling to a honey bee and take food directly from its mouth. If a hive is infested with them, several adult flies may live on a queen, but usually only one will be found on a worker. Bee lice do little damage to bee colonies, and so they are not thought of as parasites, but rather as commensal animals with bees—meaning their presence is usually tolerated by the bees. Because bee lice are killed by medications given to remove *Varroa* mites from bee colonies, they are rarely seen inside beehives. Elizabeth Evans has been keeping bees for nearly twenty years and has never seen one.

Small hive beetles

Small hive beetles, *Aethina tumida,* are the newest pest in North American beehives. First discovered in the United States in Florida in 1998, the honey-eating beetles were somehow imported from African subspecies of honey bees, where they seem to live quietly in beehives. In the European subspecies of bees that are common in the United States, small hive beetle infestations can cause serious damage to the stored honeycombs and to the honey crop. The beetle grubs (larvae) burrow through and damage the honeycombs, which results in honey running out of the combs and fermenting or becoming frothy. The larvae defecate in the honey and it becomes discolored, and because they can live in honeycombs that have been removed from beehives, they can ruin comb honey that is waiting to be extracted. It is unclear why the small hive beetle can coexist in African beehives as a minor pest but can become a serious threat in North American hives.

Question 4: Which other animals prey on bees?

Answer: The stored honey and the protein-rich brood can make a hearty meal for an animal that is equipped to steal from the hive's environment. Mice are regular marauders in honey bee colonies and will nest in a hive in winter. Larger animals and birds that attack beehives must have strong claws, tough skin, and dense hairs or feathers, especially around their mouths. In North America, skunks, raccoons, opossums, and black bears are known to do damage to beehives. Opossums and skunks will catch the sluggish wintering bees, suck them dry of honey and soft body parts, and drop their exoskeletons near the hive. In tropical rain forests in Southeast Asia, the sun bear *Helarctos malayanus,* also called a honey bear, is a known predator of beehives. Another carnivorous mammal, the honey badger *Mellivora capensis,* also feeds on bee colonies in western Asia and in Africa.

Honeyguides are birds that live in sub-Saharan Africa and parts of Asia and eat beeswax and bee brood. These birds have a fascinating technique to help them overcome the fact that they cannot typically get access to bee nests, nor can they defend themselves effectively from a honey bee attack. Although they are drab in color, it is said that honeyguides attract the attention of a larger vertebrate predator of bees (such as a sun bear, a honey badger, or even a human) using a distinctive call. The bird will then hop around, call again, and then fly a short distance away and resume calling. In this way, the honeyguide earned its name—it guides the larger mammal to a bee colony and dines on the leftovers after the mammal has endured the danger of opening the nest. One bird in this group is named

Fig. 33. There are twenty-six species of bee-eaters that feed on flying insects, primarily on honey bees. These birds are in the family Meropidae. *(Drawing by John F. Cullum.)*

Indicator indicator because of this behavior. However fascinating the stories are about these birds, their true interactions with beehive predators have not been well studied scientifically. We think these birds deserve more attention for the possibilities of interspecies communication, whether or not the bee-bird-mammal fables are true!

There is a family of migratory birds, Meropidae, that are rightfully named bee-eaters, although they also eat other flying insects. They live in southern Europe and eastward into southern Asia during the summer, but when the cold weather comes and bees stop foraging, the birds migrate to spend the winter in West Africa. There are many colorful species in this family, and they live together in large flocks, some foraging together in groups numbering in the hundreds. They chase bees and other insects and snatch them out of the air. Then they retreat to a perch with the insect in their beak, and they remove the sting from a bee or wasp before eating it by repeatedly hitting the insect on a hard surface, expelling most of its venom. There is a wonderful exhibit of bee-eaters in the San Diego Zoo.

Question 5: Does a bee heal if it gets injured?

Answer: To a limited extent, yes, bees can heal—but scientists do not have a detailed understanding of how they fight off infections. Bees do not have a well-developed immune system like the human immune system that develops antibodies against some pathogens after exposure to them. However, bees can survive the accidental removal of an antenna or part of a leg; and, although it is rare, it is possible to see bees with missing parts in an observation hive.

Question 6: Do bees get viruses or fungal infections?

Answer: There are many viruses that infect honey bees, some that have an impact on the developing brood and others that show themselves in the adults. One particular virus, aptly named the Deformed Wing Virus, results in adults with crumbled or shrunken wings. This problem only shows up in colonies that have very high levels of infection—even bees that look normal can test positive for the virus. Since the naming of colony collapse disorder in 2007, scientists are learning a lot more about viruses and how they affect bee behavior and colony health (see this chapter, question 10: What is colony collapse disorder?).

The primary fungus that affects honey bees appears in the brood but doesn't affect the adults. The infection is known as "chalkbrood" because it turns the larval bees into white, chalk-like pieces that beekeepers call "mummies." Adult bees will try to remove these dry larval remnants, and in the process they pick up spores from the fungus and accidentally spread it around the colony. Otherwise healthy colonies with good numbers of individuals in the hive can usually keep their colonies clear of chalkbrood infection, but if they are stressed by cold or wet conditions, it can become a big problem.

Question 7: How are bee diseases spread?

Answer: Insects, like humans, face a greater risk of catching and spreading diseases when they are crowded together. Biologist Adam Stow and his colleagues in Australia washed off the protective coatings from the bodies of a variety of bees that ranged from very social to solitary. They applied a solution made from each species' coating to staph bacterium, *Staphlococcus aureus,* and found that the antimicrobial coating from the most social bees was 314 times stronger than that from the most solitary bees. Even the most mildly social bees were 10 times better protected than the solitary bees.

Even though bigger colonies may tend to have better immune defenses, because there is almost constant physical contact between individuals in a colony, the risk of diseases being spread is still a major concern. Once a colony has an established infection or infestation, it is likely that nearby colonies will also show signs of disease. The actual routes of infection are often not known, but because bee diseases do spread so readily, it is assumed that foraging bees are the likely carriers. There is some evidence that bees can pick up a disease or a pathogen from a flower if they visit it after it was visited by an infected bee. When food sources are limited, honey bees sometimes will steal food from nearby colonies, and in the process they can pick up infections and bring them home.

Question 8: Do bees ever need antibiotic drugs?

Answer: There are two bacterial infections that can devastate a honey bee colony: one is called European Foul Brood (EFB) and the other is American Foul Brood (AFB). AFB is very deadly, infecting larvae that are less than three days old and causing them to die in their cells. Each infected larva contains millions of spores, and in the United Kingdom and in the United States all infected colonies are compulsorily destroyed, and movement of bees or equipment from the infected apiary is prohibited, including *all* of a beekeeper's hives, even if only one is infected. Once this infection takes hold, the bees cannot clear their colony of the stringy bacteria. There may be some variations in state and regional laws that apply.

EFB is less deadly to a colony because its bacteria does not form spores, though it can survive cold weather and continue to infect a colony the next season if it has not been eradicated. It is particularly dangerous if the colony is already under stress, but a healthy colony can be treated with an antibiotic if the infection is not too severe. To prevent infections, beekeepers will sometimes treat their colony with a powdered antibiotic called terramyacin, mixing it with sugar and shaking the powder on the inside of the colony. The risk of prophylactic treatments is that they may lead to resistant bacteria.

In the case of both infections, the larvae ingest the bacteria along with the brood food, and the bacteria then multiply rapidly in the gut of the larvae, causing death in a few days. Hive bees that clean the nest spread the infection, and even the honey becomes contaminated and spreads the disease.

Question 9: What is dysentery for a bee?

Answer: Honey bees are very clean animals and usually only eliminate wastes when they fly outside of the colony. During the winter months, cold temperatures might prevent them from flying, which can create some gastrointestinal distress for them—and a protozoan infection can begin. Evidence of these gut parasites, called *Nosema,* can be seen in the form of brown spots that appear inside and outside of the colony as the bees fly out during warm winter days and the springtime on cleansing flights to void stored wastes. The infection is usually short lasting and can be prevented through the application of a medication fed to the bees in a simple sugar syrup. There are new, more virulent strains that result in the death of colonies.

Question 10: What is colony collapse disorder?

Answer: Colony collapse disorder (CCD) is characterized by almost all of the adult worker bees flying away from their hive, abandoning the stored honey and pollen as well as their larvae and pupae. Usually all the bees leave in less than a week, and in a few cases, whole colonies have been found dead in their hives.

Beekeepers expect approximately a 20 percent loss in a normal season, but when losses are from 30 to 60 percent, as has been reported recently, there is concern that the problem can have drastic consequences for human food supplies because of the absence of pollinators to fertilize the crops. These losses have occurred as demand for pollination services has soared due to the prevalence of highly mechanized commercial farms that grow huge quantities of only one crop (monoculture). Between 1947 and 2005, colony numbers nationwide declined by over 40 percent, from 5.9 million to 2.4 million, primarily due to the accidental introduction in the 1980s of two bloodsucking parasitic mites (see this chapter, question 3: What parasites and insects prey on bees?).

Regular surveys conducted by the National Agricultural Statistics Service focus on honey production and other farming operations, but not on pollination services or colony health, so the information that has been available about these losses has not been particularly precise. The problem has been publicized as "mysterious," but, in fact, similar massive bee die-offs have been observed at least since 1869, when the first one was recorded. In 1915 when this phenomenon occurred it was called Disappearing Disease. It occurred in 1963, 1964, and 1965, and then it was called Spring Dwindling, Fall Collapse, and Autumn Collapse, respectively. The early outbreaks were localized and the causes were never determined.

There were massive bee die-offs again in 1975, 1995, 2004, and 2005, but they were overcome relatively quickly. But starting in the fall of 2006, beekeepers along the East Coast of the United States began reporting large bee losses. By February 2007 the losses had spread to some Western states until the tally reached twenty-two states in which die-offs of up to 80 percent of the colony population were reported. Recent outbreaks are being reported throughout parts of Canada and Europe.

In September 2007, a team of scientists led by Diana Cox-Foster of Pennsylvania State University reported that they had found a strong correlation between CCD and a virus from Israel that may have arrived in the United States via shipments of live bees from Australia. In 2004, it was permitted to import bees for the first time since 1922 to compensate for losses due to *Varroa* mites, and the imports came from Australia. The virus, Israeli Acute Paralysis Virus (IAPV), was identified just three years ago by researchers at Hebrew University, and it is transmitted by the *Varroa* mite. IAPV is described as a significant marker for CCD because in the recent studies it was found only in bee populations with colony collapse disorder. Although this seems like an important finding, the virus is not known to be the cause of CCD; there were many other pathogens identified in the Cox-Foster study. Their research is continuing and these results are being interpreted cautiously.

ELEVEN

Beekeeping

Question 1: Is beekeeping dangerous?

Answer: A prudent beekeeper will say that beekeeping is not dangerous, but a person who remembers a painful bee sting would probably disagree. The best answer to this question is "it depends." With careful attention to the hive and some basic knowledge of bee biology, beekeeping is not dangerous. The behavior of bees is relatively predictable; with experience, a bee-keeper can safely manage the colony and keep the bees calm. Using a smoker to puff cool smoke onto the colony before it is opened is one important step in good beekeeping. In addition to using smoke, the colony will be calmer and easier to handle if the beekeeper wears light-colored clothing and moves carefully when working around the colony. Good weather conditions, ample nectar sources, plenty of food stored in reserve in the hive, and calm bees with good genetics are other key factors that help maintain safe conditions.

The beekeeper's behavior is of prime importance, and care-lessness on the part of the beekeeper can elicit an aggressive response from the bees. The likelihood of arousing the bees and getting stung is increased by wearing dark-colored clothing or strong perfumes near the nest, moving quickly around the bees, or opening a colony during rain. Conditions that can destabilize a colony are a shortage of food, the proximity of pesticides or other chemicals, too much or too little water (water stress), disease, and overcrowding.

Fig. 34. A beekeeper, wearing a protective suit and veil, checks the health of the hive in a small colony in Pennsylvania. Note that gloves are not always necessary while working. *(Photo by Corey J. Flynn.)*

Question 2: What does a beekeeper's hive look like?

Answer: In the United States, the standard hive used by bee-keepers is called a Langstroth hive, named after the person who discovered the "bee space"—the size of the space that the bees prefer between combs (see chapter 5, question 8: What is propolis?). An important feature of the Langstroth colony is its modularity, which means that the basic features of the colony are exchangeable, replaceable, moveable, and expandable.

Essentially, the hive is a solid wooden box measuring about 16 by 20 inches long (or about 40 by 51 centimeters), and it contains ten wooden frames in which the bees build their combs. The frames hang much like hanging file folders in a file cabinet, and the depth of the box can vary from almost 6 to over 9 inches (or about 15 to 23 centimeters). Each frame is typically supplied with a vertical sheet of beeswax or beeswax-coated plastic, called foundation, which provides structure and support for the wax. In the wild, European honey bees normally build vertical sheets of wax to use for brood rearing and food storage; the bees in managed colonies build their wax over the foundation template, which becomes the bottom of the honeycomb that they build. Beekeepers call this process building out or drawing out the foundation. The wooden frames with a drawn-out foundation in place become very stable, a characteristic useful to efficient honey harvesting (see this chapter, question 6: How does a bee-keeper take honey from a hive?).

Fig. 35. A two-story Langstroth hive on the campus of Bucknell University. This colony has one tier for brood rearing and one for honey storage. *(Photo by Debra Cook-Balducci.)*

Fig. 36. In a healthy hive, worker honey bees boil out on the top of the brood frames when the hive is opened. *(Photo by Elizabeth C. Evans.)*

A single Langstroth box is called a "hive body"—a well-managed beehive typically has one or two hive bodies where the bees rear the brood and then one or two "supers" for honey storage. Brood rearing occurs on the lower tiers of the colony, while the upper tiers serve as the pantry. The bees will also store pollen in the form of bee bread and some honey around the brood nest areas. A beekeeper doesn't need to do anything to tell the bees where to rear brood or store honey—they naturally organize their colonies in this way (see color plate A).

A wooden inner cover is set on top of the supers. The inner cover is usually made of wood and fits snugly over the Langstroth box. One surface is flat, and the other has a one-half-inch outer edge. An inner cover is typically vented with either a small notch in the wooden edge or a round or oval-shaped hole in the center or both. The flat side of the inner cover is placed against the top super with very little space between it and the top bars of the frames, and this prevents the bees from building comb to fill in the gap between the inner cover and the top super. For the winter, when the bees hunker down in the hive, the inner cover is flipped upside down and the small lift around the outer edge creates an airspace that promotes air circulation and the evaporation of moisture that may accumulate. Without this space during the winter, the water in the hive could freeze and create unmanageable conditions for the bees.

Over the inner cover, an outer cover is placed over the entire top of the colony. Often made of wood covered in sheet metal or plastic, the outer cover is designed to protect the top of the hive from rain, snow, and wind. Lightweight outer covers are not typically used in locations with cold winters.

The stack of supers is set on a wooden bottom board that serves as the base of the hive, and the entire structure is usually set on a layer of cinderblocks or on a wooden stand or pallet. Keeping the beehive off the ground promotes good ventilation and prevents the colony from becoming waterlogged during rains.

Question 3: How do beehives vary in other countries?

Answer: The basic modular principles of the Langstroth hive are represented in other types of beekeeping equipment used in other countries, including the National hive in the United Kingdom, which is square, rather than rectangular, and just a bit smaller than the Langstroth hive. One of the advantages of these tiered hives is that they take advantage of the natural tendency for bees to build their colonies in a vertical fashion, with the honey being stored in the top regions of the colony and the brood nest kept toward the bottom—perhaps this organization allows the bees to regulate the space they can dedicate to building new comb to hold additional brood when necessary.

Top bar hives (TBHs) are usually longer than they are tall, and they offer an alternative style of beekeeping to the standard type described in this book. TBHs rely on moveable combs, rather than the traditional moveable frames; the combs hang

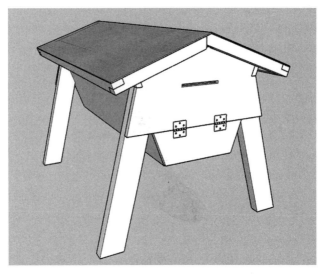

Fig. 37. Top bar hives, an alternative to the Langstroth hive, allow the bees to create free hanging combs and to develop their colonies horizontally, rather than vertically. *(Image provided by Sean Palmer.)*

down from bars across the top of the hive, and the bars fit together to make up the roof of the hive. The hive is often open underneath. These non-Langstroth hives have been used for beekeeping for hundreds of years, and they are commonly used in developing countries as they are considered less expensive to operate than traditional hives. Different management methods are required for TBHs because the combs are often destroyed when the honey is harvested. Some beekeepers believe that TBHs promote healthy bees, but to date, there haven't been many scientific studies to verify that idea.

Question 4: What is a bee skep?

Answer: A bee skep is a bell-shaped straw basket that was once used for housing bees (see color plate G). Its now familiar curved "beehive" shape was at one time a regular feature in gardens. Bees entered a skep through a small door along the bottom edge of the basket, and due to the design, the beekeeper would have to destroy the entire colony when harvesting honey from these structures. Currently, skeps are purely decorative, and in many municipalities it is illegal to keep bees in skeps or in other non-traditional hives because they are impossible to inspect for bee health. Bee skeps inspired the iconic 1960s "beehive" hairdo.

The bee skep is a metaphor for hospitality or industriousness, often used as a logo for its symbolic value. Bee skeps are well-known objects in the state of Utah because the highway signs are in the shape of a skep, and they adorn many buildings around Temple Square in Salt Lake City. In her book on bees in American history, Tammy Horn describes the symbolism of the skep for the Mormon founders of the state as a non-religious icon representing frugality, work, and faith.

Fig. 38. Popular in the 1960s, the beehive hairdo was a creation of stylist Margaret Vinci Heldt of Elmhurst, Illinois. The shape is reminiscent of a bee skep, a primitive beehive. *(Photo by Ken "Butch" Ehlers.)*

Fig. 39. Bee and beekeeping symbols are not uncommon in the United States. State roads in Utah are marked within the image of a skep, reminding drivers of the state motto, "Industry." *(Photo by Mary Capaldi Carr.)*

Question 5: How does a beekeeper manage a hive?

Answer: A beekeeper's primary tasks in hive management are to assess the behavior of the bees, to monitor and anticipate the space needed by the colony, and to treat the colony for diseases. Beekeepers have a yearly set of activities that are required for good management of their hives. During the winter, equipment is typically repaired, painted, or replaced. In the late winter, the beekeeper will assess whether the colony has enough food to last until the spring. When the bees become active with the onset of springtime, the keeper will make sure that the brood nest is being formed in the lower tiers of the colony, remove any damaged equipment, and provide food if the colony needs an extra boost. As the weather reliably warms and flowers begin to appear, the primary task becomes monitoring the space needs of the hive. Once spring arrives, a beekeeper will visit each colony at least every two weeks to check on the bees. Honey made in the spring and early summer is removed in midsummer, and this is the share of the honey for the beekeeper. The bees then have the opportunity to rebuild the honey stores they will need to sustain them through the winter from flowers that bloom in late summer and early autumn.

Question 6: How does a beekeeper take honey from a hive?

Answer: In past centuries, taking honey from wild colonies usually involved subduing the bees with smoke and breaking open the area of the hive where the colony was located. The honeycombs were torn out and destroyed along with the eggs and larvae. The honey was strained through a sieve or a basket to remove the broken pieces of comb and any other solids from the liquid honey. Modern beekeepers, however, have the benefit of moveable frame hives, and when the honey is removed using a hive tool and extracted from the honeycomb frames, the beeswax can be returned to the hive for refilling by the worker bees. Exactly how a beekeeper removes honey frames from beehives depends on the number of frames and the number of colonies that the beekeeper is managing. A hobby beekeeper may harvest just a few frames of honey, while a large beekeeping operation might harvest hundreds of frames.

The first challenge is to remove the bees from the frames of honey. A hobbyist may simply remove individual frames and use a soft bee brush to dust off the adult bees before taking the honey away, while a larger operation will use a machine, called a bee blower, that creates forced air to blow the adult worker bees off the honey frames. Many beekeepers use an alternative method of separating bees from honey, called a bee escape. This creates a one-way passage that is placed between the honey supers and the brood region below, allowing the bees to crawl downward through the escape, but not return back up. After the escape has been left in place for about twenty-four hours, the honey supers are typically bee free and can be removed without disruption of the frames. A final technique is the use of chemical bee repellents, either benzaldehyde (almond oil) or butyric anhydride (known in the beekeeping industry by its brand name, Bee-Go™). A few drops of these liquids are placed on a board that is specially designed for hive fumigation, and the board is placed for two to five minutes on top of the honey frames. The bees in the honey area will move away, and the beekeeper can take the honey off but leave the bees inside the colony. If used properly, chemical repellents are effective, but if overused, they can disrupt the entire colony.

The next task is to remove the honey from the combs. Each frame of honey is capped with a thin layer of beeswax that must be removed so that the honey can be extracted. The cappings can be removed with an uncapping fork, an uncapping knife, or another mechanical tool. Next, the frames are put into a honey extractor, which works like a large salad spinner. As the extractor rotates, the honey is forced out of the frames and down into a large holding vessel, and then the honey is usually filtered to remove large bits of wax. In some larger honey-extraction fa-

Fig. 40. A hive tool is a metal pry bar that helps beekeepers separate hive parts. It is usually painted red so that it stands out against a grassy background. (*Drawing by John F. Cullum.*)

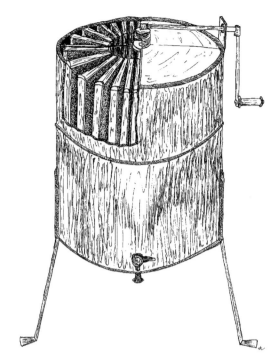

Fig. 41. A four-frame honey extractor operates via hand crank. Frames of honey spin within the chamber, spilling honey into the tank. The extracted honey is then decanted, filtered, and put into jars. (*Drawing by John F. Cullum.*)

cilities, the honey is heated so that it flows readily through the extraction and filtration process, but smaller honey extractors do not heat the honey as it is being processed.

Question 7: Can the beekeeper stop the bees from swarming?

Answer: With the use of modular beekeeping equipment, it is possible to stop bees from swarming. The bees are usually triggered to swarm because the colony is overcrowded, and if a beekeeper gives the bees extra supers to grow into, overcrowding can be controlled. Once the preparations for swarming begin (see chapter 8, question 2: What is swarming?), it is much harder to convince the bees that they don't need to swarm, and at that point just adding more space may not be enough. The beekeeper may need to put empty frames between the frames of existing combs to be sure that the bees get the message that they can stay in their nest and expand their resources into the new space.

Question 8: Why do some beekeepers clip the queen's wings?

Answer: Some beekeepers clip the queen's wings as an extra measure of bee insurance, because if the queen swarms, she will take thousands of worker bees along with her. If the queen bee cannot fly because her wings have been clipped, any swarm that forms will return to the colony. Other beekeepers don't like this practice, and they try to use good colony management to keep the bees healthy and to discourage swarming.

Question 9: Can the beekeeper put a new queen in the hive if the old one dies?

Answer: Yes, a queen can be replaced by a beekeeper, but re-queening can be a difficult process because the workers have a preference for their own queen. If the queen of a colony dies naturally, the workers will usually know that she is dying and will rear a new queen to replace her. If the queen is killed accidentally, the workers may be able to rear a replacement queen from a newly laid egg.

Under some circumstances, the beekeeper may want to replace the queen with one that has particular characteristics, such as being a better egg layer, but if a new queen is released directly into a bee colony, the workers will treat her like a stranger and forcibly remove her from the colony and possibly kill her. Normally, the guard bees learn the odor of their own colony members and prevent bees from other colonies from entering the hive. If the queen is enclosed in a small cage and introduced into a queenless colony, the bees will adjust their behavior and will come to accept her. Despite her novel odor, they will detect that she is a queen and will soon treat her as their own. Queen cages are made of wood and mesh screen, and one end has an

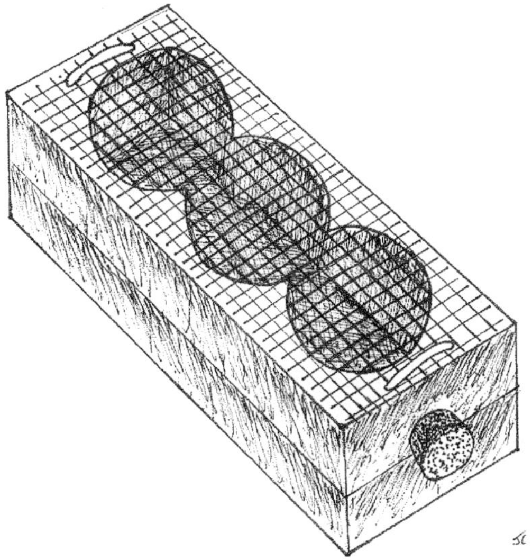

Fig. 42. A wooden queen cage has three compartments and is large enough to hold a queen and a few worker attendants. Cages hold the queen in new packages of bees and are used to re-queen a hive. (Drawing by John F. Cullum.)

exit hole drilled in the outer edge. This section is typically filled with a semi-soft sugar candy, and as the bees adjust to the new queen's odor, they eat the candy and free the queen by making it possible for her to crawl through the exit hole.

Question 10: What is a smoker?

Answer: A smoker is used by beekeepers to protect themselves from being stung by angry bees when the hive is opened to collect honey or wax. The smoker consists of a metal canister fitted with bellows and a small spout-like lid that can direct smoke in a particular direction. Beekeepers usually light a small controlled fire inside the smoker with a bit of newspaper and then burn smoke-producing kindling of dry pine needles, straw, cedar chips, or burlap.

The cool white smoke produced by the smoker pacifies the bees in a number of ways. First, the smoke triggers the bees to eat large quantities of honey, which engorges them and makes them sluggish. This behavior is probably an unlearned response that developed as bees evolved in areas where there was a risk that fire might destroy the colony; a full stomach would be useful if they were chased out of their meltable home by fire. When the bee becomes engorged, it has difficulty extending its stinger, providing another safety feature for the beekeeper. Finally, just as it is more difficult to smell a particular odor in a smoky room, the smoke also makes it harder for the bees to detect the alarm pheromones that are produced when bees are provoked. Disrupting this communication between the bees helps prevent their defensive responses to the threat presented when the beekeeper opens the hive.

Fig. 43. A small fire within a smoker generates cool smoke that calms bees. Beekeepers may burn pine needles, burlap, cardboard, or cedar chips. *(Photo by Debra Cook-Balducci.)*

Question 11: How is beeswax harvested?

Answer: Beeswax is harvested when the honey is harvested. The wax cappings removed from the honey frames are collected, melted, strained to remove impurities, and put into wax molds. While the entire honeycomb is made of wax, a beekeeper will typically return the frames containing the drawn out foundation to the hive after removing the honey from them. By doing so, the beekeeper encourages the bees to make more honey, rather than asking them to rebuild the shelves of their pantry.

Question 12: How can I start my own hive?

Answer: One of the best ways to start is to learn beekeeping with an established beekeeper before initiating a solo hive. Beekeeping organizations are common in most American communities, and most beekeepers enjoy teaching their craft to "newbees." Many beekeeping clubs and many state agricultural extension agencies offer short courses or workshops about beekeeping, and they have meetings and field days where events are scheduled for those interested in bees. Along with the activities described above, they might, for example, have a guest entomologist demonstrating bee dissection procedures to inspect for tracheal mite damage, something of great concern to beekeepers (see chapter 10, question 3: What parasites and insects prey on bees?). Some universities and colleges offer classes in beekeeping or apiculture. Appendix A provides a list of beekeeping organizations that can provide local references and resources.

There are three basic ways to start a new hive: splitting a colony, capturing a swarm, or creating a colony from a package. Actually, the latter two methods are essentially the same biologically, as a package of bees is simply just a swarm enclosed in a mesh box. Most new colonies are initiated from packages because the lineage of the queen is known and, therefore, characteristics of the bees are more predictable than those of a captured swarm that may have come from a colony with undesirable characteristics.

Beehives can be very productive in a variety of environments, but they are typically put in areas that can be warmed by the sun in the early morning and that are unlikely to be flooded. Colonies typically do best when their nest entrance faces away from the primary wind direction. There are many people who enjoy rooftop beekeeping in urban environments. A source of clean water may need to be provided by an urban beekeeper, but public parks, window boxes, and backyard gardens can provide ample food, and chances are good that nearby terraces have potted plants and flowers that are good sources of nectar and pollen. Bees can learn the location of profitable food sites and they will return to them regularly (see color plates C and D).

Question 13: Are there any reasons why people should not keep bees?

Answer: Some local governments have ordinances that prohibit beekeeping activities within certain areas, but most communities are tolerant of small-scale beekeeping operations, even in residential areas. In some arid climates, bees can become serious pests at swimming pools and care should be taken to

The Story of Brother Adam

A fragile young boy named Karl Kerhle (also written Carl Kehrle) was the son of a miller in a German village. Because of his health problems, in 1910, when he was eleven or twelve years old, his mother sent him to live at Buckfast Abbey in southwestern England. He was assigned to help tend the beehives that had been part of that Benedictine monastery since around 1882. By 1919 he joined the order and became a monk named Brother Adam, and he continued to work with the bees for over seventy-eight years, becoming internationally known as a bee expert. He wrote three books about beekeeping and was awarded the Order of the British Empire and many other honors for his work.

The Story of Brother Adam

Once he became a monk, he took over responsibility for the care of the bees, and there were serious problems. Over the prior three or four years, thirty out of the forty-six colonies at the abbey and 90 percent of the hives throughout England had been devastated by what was called Isle of Wight disease, later identified as tracheal mites. Brother Adam realized that the bees that survived the disease were all of Italian origin, and that the native British black bees, the northern variant of *Apis mellifera mellifera,* had all perished. He began using cross-breeding to develop a healthy bee population that would be a good honey producer, hardy like the black bee but disease-resistant like the Italian bee.

Brother Adam traveled all over the world to learn about native strains and to import breeding stock. Over the years, he journeyed over one hundred thousand miles, and he developed an experimental breeding program that ultimately produced the Buckfast Bee, a disease-resistant, gentle bee—a good pollen gatherer that is less inclined to swarm than many other types of honey bees. He gradually improved the strain at the abbey by crossing them with bees he discovered during his travels in Europe, the Near East, and North Africa, and Buckfast queens are still valued by beekeepers worldwide. At last count there were 240 hives that were placed in nine apiaries in the vicinity of the abbey. In 2004, over four tons of honey was produced in the abbey's immaculate and modern extraction facilities.

Brother Adam gave up his bee research in 1992 because the monastery's new abbot insisted that the main function of the abbey apiaries was honey production, not research. He was ninety-three years of age, and he died soon afterwards in 1996 at the age of ninety-eight. His three books about bee breeding and the Buckfast Bee are *In Search of the Best Strains of Bees, Beekeeping at Buckfast,* and *Breeding the Honeybee.*

provide fresh sources of water to bees in these locations. Good communication between beekeepers and their neighbors can prevent misunderstandings about the perceived dangers of bee-keeping, and annual gifts of local honey often smooth relationships between beekeepers and neighbors.

People for the Ethical Treatment of Animals (PETA), an animal rights group, refers to keeping bees as "bee slavery." Their policy statement says, in part, "honey bees are victims of unnatural living conditions, genetic manipulation, and stressful transportation." Actually, small beekeeping operations need to be respectful of the bees and careful to provide healthy conditions or their colonies will die, so their bees are generally comfortable and productive. Honey bees are a regular and important part of agriculture, and commercial beekeeping has become an industry. And like all industries, it has problems and needs some regulation to ensure the safety and fair treatment of its participants. Clearly, this issue is one with multiple perspectives, and the position of animal rights groups may not be the dominant one.

There are native bee movements in the United Kingdom (British Isles Bee Breeding Association, or BIBBA), Ireland (Galtee Bee Breeding Group), and Denmark. Their goal is to restore the original species, specifically, the British Black, the French Black, the Danish Black, and some other subspecies of honey bees. These groups want to preserve the genetic biodiversity of honey bee breeds and to use the original lineages to artificially select for desirable traits. This process may produce more gentle bees or bees with the ability to resist infection.

Question 14: How can I safely observe bees?

Answer: Beekeepers and their families often bring samples of their honey to be judged competitively at state and county fairs, and they sometimes bring a hive full of bees along as well. They may demonstrate such bee-related activities as candle dipping, candle-making with wax molds, honey extraction, bee dances, and mead making (see chapter 7, question 9: What is mead?).

Fig. 44. Bee scientist Dr. Jeri Wright with a "bee bikini," demonstrating that "bee beards" aren't the only way that beekeepers can manipulate a swarm of honey bees. (*Photo by Jodi Miller.*)

One especially dramatic demonstration is a person with a beard made of living bees. Bottled queen pheromone is applied to the person's face to attract bees in a controlled swarm, giving the appearance of a beard. In the old days, an actual queen in a specially constructed cage was fitted to the chin and then hidden by the swarm that came to surround their queen. Though this stunt looks dangerous, the bees aren't inclined to sting when they sense the presence of their queen.

Many zoos, botanical gardens, garden centers, and plant conservatories have observation colonies in indoor exhibits so that visitors can appreciate the activities of bees without fear of being stung. An observation colony is essentially a beehive sandwiched between two thick panes of glass, where the bees live on frames set into the hive, just as they would in a conventional beekeeper's hive. The bees go about their business as usual, caring for the queen and flying to and from the colony through a port in the wall of the hive. Many features of bee biology have been identified by researchers using this type of structure.

Bee Organizations

American Beekeeping Federation, http://www.abfnet.org

American Honey Producers Association, http://www.americanhoney
producers.org

Eastern Apiculture Society (EAS), http://www.easternapiculture.org

Entomological Society of America, http://www.entsoc.org/

4 H Clubs, http://www.4-h.org

Mid-Atlantic Apiculture Research and Extension Consortium
(MAAREC), http://maarec.cas.psu.edu

National Council for Agricultural Education, http://www.agedhq.org/
councilindex.cfm

National FFA Organization (originally the Future Farmers of America), http://www.ffa.org

National Honey Board, http://www.honey.com

North American Pollinator Protection Campaign, http://www.nappc
.org

Sonoran Arthropod Studies Institute, http://www.sasionline.org

State Honey and Beekeeping Organizations, http://www.honeyo.com/
org-US_State.shtml

U.S. Department of Agriculture Cooperative State Research, Education and Extension Service, http://www.csrees.usda.gov

Western Apiculture Society (WAS), http://groups.ucanr.org/WAS/

Xerces Society, http://www.xerces.org

Young Entomologists' Society, http://members.aol.com/yesbugs/
bugclub.html

Suggestions for Further Reading

Books

Bowling, A. C. 2006. *Complementary and alternative medicine and multiple sclerosis.* New York: Demos Medical Publishing, LLC.

Coggshall, W. L., and R. A. Morse. 1984. *Beeswax: Production, harvesting, processing, and products.* Cheshire, CT: Wicwas Press.

Crane, E. 1999. *The world history of beekeeping and honey hunting.* London, U.K.: Taylor & Francis.

Day, L., et al., 2007. *Field guide to the natural world of New York City.* Baltimore, MD: Johns Hopkins University Press.

Delaplane, K. S., and D. F. Mayer. 2000. *Crop pollination by bees.* New York: CABI Publishing.

Goulson, D. 2003. *Bumblebees: Their behaviour and ecology.* New York: Oxford University Press.

Horn, T. 2005. *Bees in America: How the honey bee shaped a nation.* Lexington: University Press of Kentucky.

Hubbell, S. 1988. *A book of bees.* New York: Houghton Mifflin.

Kidd, S. M. 2002. *The secret life of bees.* New York: Penguin Books.

Langstroth, L. L. 2004. *Langstroth's hive and the honey-bee: The classic beekeeper's manual.* New York: Courier Dover Publications.

Michener, C. D. 2000. *The bees of the world.* Baltimore, MD: Johns Hopkins University Press.

Mizrahi, A., and Y. Lensky. 1997. *Bee products: Properties, applications, and apitherapy.* New York: Springer.

Morse, R. A., and K. Flottum. 1990. *The ABC & XYZ of bee culture.* 40th ed. Medina, OH: A. I. Root Co.

Morse, R. A., and R. Nowogrodzki. 1990. *Honey bee pests, predators, and diseases.* Ithaca, NY: Cornell University Press.

National Research Council (U.S.). 2007. *Status of pollinators in North America.* Washington, DC: National Academies Press.

Oldroyd, B. P., and S. Wongsiri. 2006. *Asian honey bees: Biology, conservation, and human interactions*. Cambridge, MA: Harvard University Press.

Opton, G., and N. Hughes. 2000. *Honey: A connoisseur's guide with recipes*. Berkeley, CA: Ten Speed Press.

Oster, G. F., and E. O. Wilson. 1978. *Caste and ecology in the social insects*. Princeton, NJ: Princeton University Press.

Roubik, D. W. 1992. *Ecology and natural history of tropical bees*. New York: Cambridge University Press.

Sammataro, D., and A. Avitabile. 1998. *The beekeeper's handbook: A teaching text for beginners to advanced beekeepers*. Ithaca, NY: Cornell University Press.

Seeley, T. D. 1996. *The wisdom of the hive: The social physiology of bee colonies*. Cambridge, MA: Harvard University Press.

Waser, N. M., and J. Ollerton. 2006. *Plant-pollinator interactions: From specialization to generalization*. Chicago: University of Chicago Press.

Winston, M. L. 1987. *The biology of the honey bee*. Cambridge, MA: Harvard University Press.

Web sites

Honey Bee Research at the University of Illinois at Urbana-Champaign, http://www.life.uiuc.edu/robinson/

Mid-Atlantic Apiculture Research and Education Consortium, http://maarec.cas.psu.edu/

North American Pollinator Protection Campaign, http://www.nappc.org/

Pollinator Conservation Program with the Xerces Society, http://www.xerces.org/Pollinator_Insect_Conservation/

USDA Agricultural Research Service—Carl Hayden Bee Research Center, Tuscon, Arizona, USA, http://gears.tucson.ars.ag.gov/dept/about.html

USDA Agricultural Research Service—Honey Bee Breeding, Genetics, and Physiology Research Laboratory, Baton Rouge, Louisiana, USA, http://www.ars.usda.gov/Main/site_main.htm?modecode=64-13-30-00

USDA Agricultural Research Service Bee Biology and Systematics Laboratory, Logan, Utah, USA, http://www.loganbeelab.usu.edu

USDA Agricultural Research Service Bee Laboratory, Beltsville, Maryland, USA, http://www.ars.usda.gov/main/site_main.htm?modecode=12-75-05-00

References

Chapter 1: Bee Basics

Question 3: How many species of bees exist?

Mateus, S., and F. B. Noll. 2004. Predatory behavior in a necrophagous bee Trigona hypogea (Hymenoptera; Apidae, Meliponini). *Naturwissenschaften* 91:94–96.

Roubik, D. W. 1982. Obligate necrophagy in a social bee. *Science* 217:1059–1060.

Question 4: How are bees classified?

Arnett, R. H. 2000. American insects: *A handbook of the insects of America north of Mexico*. Boca Raton, FL: CRC Press.

Castner, J. L. 2000. *Photographic atlas of entomology and guide to insect identification*. Gainesville, FL: Feline Press.

Danforth, B. N., et al. 2006. The history of early bee diversification based on five genes plus morphology. *Proceedings of the National Academy of Sciences* 103:15118–15123.

Kaplan, N., and M. Linial. 2006. ProtoBee: Hierarchical classification and annotation of the honey bee proteome. *Genome Research* 16:1431–1438.

McClung, R. M. 1971. *Bees, wasps, and hornets and how they live*. New York: William Morrow.

Michener, C. D. 1974. *The social behavior of the bees, a comparative study*. Cambridge, MA: Harvard University Press.

Pennisi, E. 2006. Honey bee genome illuminates insect evolution and social behavior. *Science* 314:578–579.

Rubin, E. B., et al. 2006. Molecular and phylogenetic analyses reveal mammalian-like clockwork in the honey bee (*Apis mellifera*) and shed new light on the molecular evolution of the circadian clock. *Genome Research* 16:1352–1365.

Question 5: What is the earliest evidence of the existence of bees?

Engel, M. S., and D. Grimaldi. 2005. *Evolution of the insects.* New York: Cambridge University Press.

Mitchener, C. D,. and D. Grimaldi. 1988. The oldest fossil bee: Apoid history, evolutionary stasis, and antiquity of social behavior. *Proceedings of the National Academy of Science* 85:6424–6426.

Poinar, G. O., Jr., and B. N. Danforth. 2006. A fossil bee from early cretaceous Burmese amber. *Science* 314:614.

Whitfield, C. W., et al. 2006. Thrice out of Africa: Ancient and recent expansions of the honey bee, *Apis mellifera. Science* 314:642–645.

Question 7: Do all bees make honey?

Engel, M.S. 1999. The taxonomy of recent and fossil honey bees (Hymenoptera: Apidae: *Apis*). *Journal of Hymenoptera Research* 8:165–196.

Question 8: Are there different types of bees within one hive of honey bees?

Beekman, M., and B. P. Oldroyd. 2006. When workers disunite: Intraspecific parasitism by eusocial bees. *Annual Review of Entomology* 53:19–37.

Question 9: What is the role of the workers?

Ament, S. A., et al. 2008. Insulin signaling is involved in the regulation of worker division of labor in honey bee colonies. *Proceedings of the National Academy of Sciences* 105:4226–4231.

Beekman, M., and B. P. Oldroyd. 2006. When workers disunite: Intraspecific parasitism by eusocial bees. *Annual Review of Entomology* 53:19–37.

Beggs, K. T., et al. 2007. Queen pheromone modulates brain dopamine function in worker honey bees. *Proceedings of the National Academy of Sciences* 104:2460–2464.

Drapeau, M. D., et al. 2006. Evolution of the yellow/major royal jelly protein family and the emergence of social behavior in honey bees. *Genome Research* 16:1385–1394.

Pierce, A. L., L. A. Lewis, and S. S. Schneider. 2007. The use of the vibration signal and worker piping to influence queen behavior during swarming in honey bees, *Apis mellifera. Ethology* 113:267–275.

Ravary, F., et al. 2007. Individual experience alone can generate lasting division of labor in ants. *Current Biology* 17:1308–1312.

Whitfield, C. W., A. Cziko, and G. E. Robinson. 2003. Gene expression profiles in the brain predict behavior in individual honey bees. *Science* 302:296–299.

Whitfield, C. W., et al. 2006. Genomic dissection of behavioral maturation in the honey bee. *Proceedings of the National Academy of Sciences* 103:16068–16075.

Question 11: What is the role of the queen?

Jordan, L. A., et al. 2008. Cheating honeybee workers produce royal offspring. *Proceedings of the Royal Society B: Biological Sciences* 275:345–351.

Lattorff, H.M.G., et al. 2007. Control of reproductive dominance by the *thelytoky* gene in honeybees. *Biology Letters* 3:292–295.

Chapter 2: Bee Bodies

Question 1: How does a honey bee develop from an egg to an adult?

Jones, J. C., et al. 2005. The effects of rearing temperature on developmental stability and learning and memory in the honey bee, *Apis mellifera. Journal of Comparative Physiology A: Neuroethology, Sensory, Neural, and Behavioral Physiology* 191:1121–1129.

Question 3: What do bees eat?

Borrell, B. J. 2004. Suction feeding in orchid bees (Apidae: Euglossini). *Proceedings of the Royal Society B: Biological Sciences, Biology Letters Supplement* 271:S164-S166.

Kryger, P., U. Kryger, and F. A. Moritz. 2000. Genotypical variability for the tasks of water collecting and scenting in a honey bee colony. *Ethology* 106:769–779.

Visscher, P. K., K. Crailsheim, and G. Sherman. 1996. How do honey bees (*Apis mellifera*) fuel their water foraging flights? *Journal of Insect Physiology* 42:1089–1094.

Question 4: How long do bees live?

Amdam, G. V., and R. E. Page Jr. 2005. Intergenerational transfers may have decoupled physiological and chronological age in a eusocial insect. *Aging Research Reviews* 4:398–408.

Corona, M., et al. 2007. Vitellogenin, juvenile hormone, insulin signaling, and queen honey bee longevity. *Proceedings of the National Academy of Sciences* 104:7128–7133.

Omholt, S. W., and G. V. Amdam. 2004. Epigenetic regulation of aging in honeybee workers. *Science of Aging Knowledge Environment* 26:28.

Remolina, S. C., et al. 2007. Senescence in the worker honey bee *Apis mellifera. Journal of Insect Physiology* 53:1027–1033.

Sen Sarma, M., C. W. Whitfield, and G. E. Robinson. 2007. Species differences in brain gene expression profiles associated with adult behavioral maturation in honey bees. *BMC Genomics* 8:202.

Sullivan, J. P., et al. 2003. Juvenile hormone and division of labor in honey bee colonies: Effects of allatectomy on flight behavior and metabolism. *Journal of Experimental Biology* 206:2287–2296.

Whitfield, C. W., A. Cziko, and G. E. Robinson. 2003. Gene expression profiles in the brain predict behavior in individual honey bees. *Science* 302:296–299.

Question 5: Are bees intelligent?

Fahrbach, S. E. 2006. Structure of the mushroom bodies of the insect brain. *Annual Review of Entomology* 51:209–232

Giurfa, M., et al. 2001. The concepts of sameness and difference in an insect. *Nature* 410:930–933.

Menzel, R., and M. Giurfa. 2006. Dimensions of cognition in an insect, the honeybee. *Behavioral and Cognitive Neuroscience Reviews* 5:24–40.

Stach, S., J. Bernard, and M. Giurfa. 2004. Local-feature assembling in visual pattern recognition and generalization in honeybees. *Nature* 429:758–761.

Virtual Atlas of the Honeybee. On the Web site Freie Universitat Berlin. See http://www.neurobiologie.fu-berlin.de/beebrain/. Accessed July 26, 2008.

Withers, G. S., S. E. Fahrbach, and G. E. Robinson. 1993. Selective neuroanatomical plasticity and division of labour in the honey bee. *Nature* 364:238–240.

———. 1995. Effect of experience on the organization of the mushroom bodies of honey bees. *Journal of Neurobiology* 26:130–144.

Question 7: Do bees bleed?

Evans, D. L., and J. O. Schmidt, eds. 1990. *Insect defenses: Adaptive mechanisms and strategies of prey and predators.* Albany: State University of New York Press.

Hayes, J. 1998. *The classroom.* Hamilton, IL: Dadant and Sons.

Question 9: What do bees see?

Chittka, L., and N. E. Raine. 2006. Recognition of flowers by pollinators. *Current Opinion in Plant Biology* 9:428–435.

Dyer, A. G., C. Neumeyer, and L. Chittka. 2005. Honeybee (*Apis mellifera*) vision can discriminate between and recognise images of human faces. *Journal of Experimental Biology* 208:4709–4714.

Dyer, A. G., M.G.P. Rosa, and D. H. Reser. 2008. Honeybees can recognise images of complex natural scenes for use as potential landmarks. *Journal of Experimental Biology* 211:1180–1186.

Hanlon, M. A bees-eye view: How insects see flowers very differently to us. On the Web site Daily Mail. See http://www.dailymail.co.uk/pages/live/articles/technology/technology.html?in_article_id=473897. Accessed April 4, 2008.

Kastberger, G. 2008. The ocelli control the flight course in honey bees. *Physiological Entomology* 15(3):337–346.

Wakakuwa, M., et al. 2005. Spectral heterogeneity of honeybee ommatidia. *Naturwissenschaften* 92:464–467.

Wehner, R., and G. D. Bernard. 1993. Photoreceptor twist: A solution to the false-color problem. *Proceedings of the National Academy of Sciences* 90:4132–4135.

Williams, S. K., and A. G. Dyer. 2007. A photographic simulation of insect vision. *Journal of Ophthalmic Photography* 29:10–14.

Williams, S. K., D. Reiser, and A. G. Dyer. 2008. A biologically inspired mechano-optical imaging system based on insect vision. *Journal of Biocommunication* 34:e3-e7.

Question 10: Do bees have bones?

Couvillon, M. J., et al. 2007. Nest-mate recognition template of guard honeybees (*Apis mellifera*) is modified by wax comb transfer. *Biology Letters* 3:228–230.

Question 11: How do bees' wings work?

Danforth, B. N. 1991. The morphology and behavior of dimorphic males in *Perdita portalis* (Hymenoptera: Andrenidae). *Behavioral Ecology and Sociobiology* 29:235–247.

———. 1999. Emergence dynamics and bet hedging in a desert bee, *Perdita portalis*. *Proceedings of the Royal Society B: Biological Sciences* 266:1985–1994.

Question 13: How do bees hold onto slippery surfaces?

Dade, H. A. 1962. *Anatomy and dissection of the honeybee*. London: Bee Research Association.

Jarau, S., et al. 2005. Morphology and structure of the tarsal glands of the stingless bee *Melipona seminigra*. *Naturwissenschaften* 92:147–150.

Lensky, Y., et al. 1985. The fine structure of the tarsal glands of the honeybee *Apis mellifera* (Hymenoptera). *Cell and Tissue Research* 240:153–158.

Chapter 3: Bee Behavior

Question 1: Can a bee hear?

Kirchner, W. H., C. Dreller, and W. F. Towne. 1991. Hearing in honeybees: Operant conditioning and spontaneous reactions to airborne sound. *Journal of Comparative Physiology A: Neuroethology, Sensory, Neural, and Behavioral Physiology* 168:85–89.

Towne, W. F. 1994. Frequency discrimination in the hearing of honey bees (Hymenoptera: Apidae). *Journal of Insect Behavior* 8:281–286.

Tsujiuchi, S., et al. 2007. Dynamic range compression in the honey bee auditory system toward waggle dance sounds. *PLoS ONE* 2:e234.

Question 2: Is taste important to a bee?

Biesmeijer, J. C., et al. 1999. Niche differentiation in nectar-collecting stingless bees: The influence of morphology, floral choice and interference competition. *Ecological Entomology* 24:380–388.

Burns, J. G. 2005. Impulsive bees forage better: The advantage of quick, sometimes inaccurate foraging decisions. *Animal Behaviour* 70:e1–e5.

Chittka, L., and J. Spaethe. 2007. Visual search and the importance of time in complex decision making by bees. *Arthropod-Plant Interactions* 1:37–44.

Chittka, L., J. D. Thomson, and N. M. Waser. 1999. Flower constancy, insect psychology, and plant evolution. *Naturwissenschaften* 86:361–377.

Gegear, R. J., and J. G.Burns. 2007. The birds, the bees, and the virtual flowers: Can pollinator behavior drive ecological speciation in flowering plants? *American Naturalist* 170:551–566.

Petanidou, T. 2005. Sugars in Mediterranean floral nectars: An ecological and evolutionary approach. *Journal of Chemical Ecology* 31:1573–1561.

Robertson, H. M., and K. W. Wanner. 2006. The chemoreceptor superfamily in the honey bee *Apis mellifera:* Expansion of the odorant, but not gustatory, receptor family. *Genome Research* 16:1395–1403.

Sargent, R. D. 2006. The role of local species abundance in the evolution of pollinator attraction in flowering plants. *American Naturalist* 167:67–80.

Question 3: How do hungry bees share food?

Gil, M., and R. J. De Marco. Olfactory learning by means of trophallaxis in *Apis mellifera. Journal of Experimental Biology* 208:671–680.

Goyret, J., and W. M. Farina. 2004. Descriptive study of anntennation during trophallactic unloading contacts in honeybees *Apis mellifera carnica*. *Insectes Sociaux* 50:274–276.

Hubbell, S. 1988. *A book of bees*. Boston: Houghton Mifflin.

Question 4: How do bees keep themselves clean?

Bozic, J., and T. Valentincic. 1995. Quantitative analysis of social grooming behavior of the honey bee *Apis mellifera carnica*. *Apidologie* 26:141–147.

Danka, R. G., and J. D. Villa. 2004. Bees that resist mites are busy groomers. *Agricultural Research Magazine* 52:21.

Harder, L. D. 1990. Behavioral responses by bumble bees to variation in pollen availability. *Oecologia* 85:41–47.

Land, B. B., and T. D. Seeley. 2004. The grooming invitation dance of the honey bee. *Ethology* 110:1–10.

Moore, D., et al. 1995. A highly specialized social grooming honey bee (Hymenoptera: Apidae). *Journal of Insect Behavior* 8:855–860.

Rademaker, M.C.J., T. J. De Jong, and P.G.L. Klinkhamer. 1997. Pollen dynamics of bumblebee visitation on *Echium vulgare*. *Functional Ecology* 11:554–563.

Ruttner, F., and H. Hanel. 1992. Active defense against varroa mites in a carniolan strain of honey bees (*Apis mellifera carnica* Pollman). *Apidologie* 23:173–187.

Thomson, J. D. 1986. Pollen transport and deposition by bumble bees in *Erythronium:* Influences of floral nectar and bee grooming. *Journal of Ecology* 74:329–341.

Question 6: How do bees communicate?

Barron, A. B., et al. 2007. Octopamine modulates honey bee dance behavior. *Proceedings of the National Academy of Sciences* 104:1703–1707.

Beekman, M., and B. P. Oldroyd. 2006. When workers disunite: Intraspecific parasitism by eusocial bees. *Annual Review of Entomology* 53:19–37.

Breed, M. D. 1998. Recognition pheromones of the honey bee. *Bioscience* 48:463–470.

Couvillon, M. J., et al. 2007. Nest-mate recognition template of guard honeybees (*Apis mellifera*) is modified by wax comb transfer. *Biology Letters* 3:228–230.

Grüter, C., M. S. Balbuena, and W. M. Farina. 2008. Informational conflicts created by the waggle dance. *Proceedings of the Royal Society B, Biological Sciences* 275:1321–1327.

Michelsen, A., W. H. Kirchner, and M. Lindauer. 1986. Sound and vibrational signals in the dance language of the honeybee, *Apis mellifera*. *Behavioral Ecology and Sociobiology* 18:207–212.

Pastor, K. A., and T. D. Seeley. 2005. The brief piping signal of the honey bee: Begging call or stop signal? *Ethology* 111:775–784.

Pflumm, W., and K. Wilhelm. 1982. Olfactory feedback in the scent marking behaviour of foraging honeybees at the food source? *Physiological Entomology* 7:203–207.

Pierce, A. L., L. A. Lewis, and S. S. Schneider. 2007. The use of the vibration signal and worker piping to influence queen behavior during swarming in honey bees, *Apis mellifera*. *Ethology* 113:267–275.

Ribbands, C. R. 1955. The scent perception of the honeybee. *Proceedings of the Royal Society B: Biological Sciences* 143:367–379.

Robertson, H. M., and K. W. Wanner. 2006. The chemoreceptor superfamily in the honey bee *Apis mellifera:* Expansion of the odorant, but not gustatory, receptor family. *Genome Research* 16:1395–1403.

Schneider, S. 2007. Migration dance; Vibration signal. In *The ABC & XYZ of bee culture*, 41st ed., ed. H. Shimanuki, K. Flottum, and A. Harman, 183–184. Medina, OH: A. I. Root.

Schneider, S. S., and L. A. Lewis. 2004. The vibrational signal, modulatory communication and the organization of labor in honey bees, *Apis mellifera*. *Apidologie* 35:117–131.

Seeley, T. D., and P. K. Visscher. 2003. Choosing a home: How the scouts in a honey bee swarm perceive the completion of their group decision making. *Behavioral Ecology and Sociobiology* 54:511–520.

Su, Songkun, et al. 2008. East learns from west: Asiatic honeybees can understand dance language of European honeybees. *PLoS ONE* 3: e2365.

Thom, C., D. C. Gilley, and J. Tautz. 2004. Worker piping in honey bees (*Apis mellifera*): The behavior of piping nectar foragers. *Behavioral Ecology and Sociobiology* 53:199–205.

von Frisch, K. 1967. *The dance language and orientation of bees.* Cambridge, MA: Harvard University Press.

Question 8: What is piping behavior?

Pierce, A. L., L .A. Lewis, and S. S. Schneider. 2007. The use of the vibration signal and worker piping to influence queen behavior during swarming in honey bees, *Apis mellifera*. *Ethology* 113:267–275.

Seeley, T. D., and J. Tautz. 2001. Worker piping in honey bee swarms and its role in preparing for liftoff. *Journal of Comparative Physiology A: Neuroethology, Sensory, Neural, and Behavioral Physiology* 187: 667–676.

von Frisch, K. 1967. *The dance language and orientation of bees*. Cambridge, MA: Harvard University Press.

Winston, M. L. 1987. *The biology of the honey bee*. Cambridge, MA: Harvard University Press.

Question 9: Can bees tell time?

Hodge, C. F. 1894. Death: Observations on man and honey-bee. *Journal of Physiology* 17:128–134.

Lindauer, M. 1971. *Communication among social bees*. Cambridge, MA: Harvard University Press.

Shemesh, Y., M. Cohen, and G. Bloch. 2007. The natural plasticity in circadian rhythms is mediated by reorganization in the molecular clockwork in honeybees. *FASEB Journal* 21:2304–2311.

Toma, D. P., et al. 2000. Changes in period mRNA levels in the brain and division of labor in honey bee colonies. *Proceedings of the National Academy of Science* 97:6914–6919.

Question 10: Do bees sleep?

Kaiser, W. 1988. Busy bees need rest, too—behavioural and electromyographical sleep signs in honeybees. *Journal of Comparative Physiology A: Neuroethology, Sensory, Neural, and Behavioral Physiology* 163: 565–584.

Klein, B. A. 2006. Caste-dependent sleep of worker honey bees. *Journal of Experimental Biology* 211:3028–3040.

Klein, B. A., and T. D. Seeley. 2007. Work schedules impact sleep schedules in foraging honey bees. *Sleep Abstracts* 30:A38.

Sauer, S., E. Hermann, and W. Kaiser. 2004. Sleep deprivation in honey bees. *Journal of Sleep Research* 13:145–152.

Shaw, P. 2003. Awakening to the behavioral analysis of sleep in *Drosophilia. Journal of Biological Rhythms* 18:4–11.

Southwick, E. E. 1991. Bee sleep. *American Bee Journal* 131:165–166.

Question 11: Do bees perceive magnetic fields?

Bitterman, M. E. 1989. Attached magnets impair magnetic field discrimination by honeybees. *Journal of Experimental Biology* 141: 447–451.

Gould, J. L., J. L. Kirschvink, and K. S. Deffeyes. 1978. Bees have magnetic remanence. *Science* 201:1026–1028.

Hsu, C., and C. Li. 1994. Magnetoreception in honeybees. *Science* 265:95–97.

Keim, C. N., et al. 2002. Ferritin in iron containing granules from the fat body of the honeybees *Apis mellifera* and *Scaptotrigona postica. Micron* 33:53–59.

Nichol, H., and M. Locke. 1995. Honeybees and magnetoreception. *Science* 269:1888–1889.

Question 12: How do bees navigate?

Brockman, A., and G. E. Robinson. 2007. Central projections of sensory systems involved in honey bee dance language communication. *Brain, Behavior and Evolution* 70:125–136.

Capaldi, E. A., and F. C. Dyer. 1999. The role of orientation flights on homing performance in honey bees. *Journal of Experimental Biology* 202:1655–1666.

Dyer, A. G., M.G.P. Rosa, and D. H. Reser. 2008. Honeybees can recognize images of complex natural scenes for use as potential landmarks. *Journal of Experimental Biology* 211:1180–1186.

Giurfa, M., and E. A. Capaldi. 1999. Vectors, routes and maps: New findings about navigation in insects. *Trends in Neurosciences* 22:237–242.

Gould, J. 2004. Animal navigation. *Current Biology* 14:R221-R224.

Lehrer, M. 1997. Honeybees visual spatial orientation at the feeding site. In *Orientation and Communication in Arthropods,* ed. M. Lehrer, 115–144. New York: Springer.

Srinivasan, M. V., et al. 2000. Honeybee navigation: Nature and calibration of the "odometer." *Science* 287:851–853.

von Frisch, K. 1967. *The dance language and orientation of bees.* Cambridge, MA: Harvard University Press.

Wei, C. A., S. L. Rafalko, and F. C. Dyer. 2002. Deciding to learn: Modulation of learning flights in honeybees, *Apis mellifera. Journal of Comparative Physiology A: Neuroethology, Sensory, Neural, and Behavioral Physiology* 188:725–737.

Question 13: How do bees sense and use polarized light?

Capaldi, E., and F. Dyer. 1999. The role of orientation flights on homing performance in honeybees. *Journal of Experimental Biology* 202:1655–1666.

Collett, T. S., et al. 1992. Visual landmarks and route following in desert ants. *Journal of Comparative Physiology A: Neuroethology, Sensory, Neural, and Behavioral Physiology* 170:435–442.

Dyer, F. 1996. Spatial memory and navigation by honeybees on the scale of the foraging range. *Journal of Experimental Biology* 199:147–154.

Kevan, P. G., L. Chittka, and A. Dyer. 2001. Limits to the salience of ultraviolet: Lessons from colour vision in bees and birds. *Journal of Experimental Biology* 204:2571–2580.

Lambrinos, D., et al. 1997. An autonomous agent navigating with a polarized lightcompass. *Adaptive Behavior* 6:131–161.

Rossel, S., and R. Wehner. 1986. Polarization vision in bees. *Nature* 323:128–131.

Wakakuwa, M., et al. 2005. Spectral heterogeneity of honeybee ommatidia. *Naturwissenschaften* 92:464–467.

Wehner, R. 1989. Neurobiology of polarization vision. *Trends in Neurosciences* 12:353–359.

Wehner, R., B. Michel, and P. Antonsen. 1996. Visual navigation in insects: Coupling of egocentric and geocentric information. *Journal of Experimental Biology* 199:129–140.

Wehner, R., and S. Strasser. 1985. The POL area of the honey bee's eye: Behavioural evidence. *Physiological Entomology* 10:337–349.

Question 14: Do bees ever get fooled by predators?

Brower, L. P., J. Van Zandt Brower, and P. W. Westcott. 1960. Experimental studies of mimicry 5. The reactions of toads (*Bufo terrestris*) to bumblebees (*Bombus americanorum*) and their robberfly mimics (*Mallophora bomboides*), with a discussion of aggressive mimicry. *American Naturalist* 94:343–355.

Hafernik, J., and L. Saul-Gershenz. 2000. Beetle larvae cooperate to mimic bees. *Nature* 405:35–36.

Pasteur, G. 1982. A classificatory review of mimicry systems. *Annual Review of Ecology and Systematics* 13:169–199.

Rettenmeyer, C. W. 1970. Insect mimicry. *Annual Review of Entomology* 15:43–74.

Robinson, M. H. 1969. Predatory behavior of *Argiope argentata* (Fabricius). *American Zoologist* 1:161–173.

Saul-Gershenz, L., and J. G. Millar. 2006. Phoretic nest parasites use sexual deception to obtain transport to their host's nest. *Proceedings of the National Academy of Sciences* 103:14039–14044.

Thery, M., and J. Casas. 2002. Predator and prey views of spider camouflage. *Nature* 415:10.

Chapter 4: Bee Love

Question 1: How does a bee attract a mate?

Robertson, H. M., and K. W. Wanner. 2006. The chemoreceptor superfamily in the honey bee, *Apis mellifera:* Expansion of the odorant, but not gustatory, receptor family. *Genome Research* 16:1395–1404.

Sugiura, S., et al. 2007. Flower-visiting behavior of male bees is triggered by nectar-feeding insects. *Naturwissenschaften* 94:703–707.

Question 2: Do all bees mate?

Beekman, M., and B. P. Oldroyd. 2006. When workers disunite: Intraspecific parasitism by eusocial bees. *Annual Review of Entomology* 53:19–37.

Question 3: How do bees mate?

Dade, H. A. 1962. *Anatomy and dissection of the honeybee*. London: Bee Research Association.

Jones, J.C., et al. 2004. Honey bee nest thermoregulation: Diversity promotes stability. *Science* 305:402–404.

Winston, M. 1987. *The biology of the honey bee*. Cambridge, MA: Harvard University Press.

Question 4: Why does a queen mate with more than one drone?

Jones, J. Genetic differences among honey bees (*Apis Mellifera*) performing the task of thermoregulation. On the Web site Behavior and Genetics of Social Insects Laboratory, University of Sydney. See http://www.bio.usyd.edu.au/Social_InsectsLab/Julia/Julia.htm. Accessed April 5, 2008.

Mattila, H. R., and T. D. Seeley. 2007. Genetic diversity in honey bee colonies enhances productivity and fitness. *Science* 317:362–364.

Schmid-Hempel, P., and B. Baer. 1999. Experimental variation in polyandry affects parasite loads and fitness in a bumblebee. *Nature* 397:151–154.

Seeley, T. D., and D. R. Tarpy. 2006. Queen promiscuity lowers disease within honeybee colonies. *Proceedings of the Royal Society B: Biological Sciences* 274:67–72.

Question 6: How is the sex of a bee determined?

Beye, M., et al. 2003. The gene *csd* is the primary signal for sexual development in the honeybee and encodes an SR-type protein. *Cell* 114:1–20.

Cho, S., et al. 2006. Evolution of the complementary sex-determination gene of honey bees: Balancing selection and trans-species polymorphisms. *Genome Research* 16:1366–1375.

Evans, J. D., et al. 2004. Molecular basis of sex determination in haplodiploids. *Trends in Ecology and Evolution* 19:1–3.

Question 7: What is royal jelly and how does it produce a queen?

Corona, M., E. Estrada, and M. Zurita. 1999. Differential expression of mitochondrial genes between queens and workers during caste determination in the honeybee *Apis mellifera*. *Journal of Experimental Biology* 202:929–938.

Koywiwattrakul, P., et al. 2005. Effects of carbon dioxide narcosis on ovary development and gene expression in worker honey bees. *Journal of Insect Science* 5:36.

Kucharski, R., et al. 2008. Nutritional control of reproductive status in honeybees via DNA methylation. *Science* 319:1827–1830.

Question 10: Can bees be instrumentally inseminated?

The Development of Honeybee Artificial Insemination. On the Web site Apiculture Program, Department of Entomology, North Carolina State University. See http://www.cals.ncsu.edu/entomology/apiculture/PDF%20files/2.14.pdf. Accessed April 5, 2008.

Honey bee artificial insemination instrument. On the Web site Chung Jin Biotech Co. Ltd. See http://younan99.en.ecplaza.net/catalog.asp?DirectoryID=81469&CatalogID=197772. Accessed April 5, 2008.

Laidlaw, H. H., Jr. 1977. *Instrumental insemination of honey bee queens*. Hamilton, IL: Dandant.

Chapter 5: Bees in the Hive

Question 3: What do bees do all day?

Hodge, C. F. 1894. Death: Observations on man and honey-bee. *Journal of Physiology* 17:128–134.Kaiser, W. 1988. Busy bees need rest, too—behavioural and electromyographical sleep signs in honeybees. *Journal of Comparative Physiology A: Neuroethology, Sensory, Neural, and Behavioral Physiology* 163:565–584.

Klein, B. A., and T. D. Seeley. 2007. Work schedules impact sleep schedules in foraging honey bees. *Sleep Abstracts* 30:A38.

Lindauer, M. 1971. *Communication among social bees*. Cambridge, MA: Harvard University Press.

Sauer, S., E. Hermann, and W. Kaiser. 2004. Sleep deprivation in honey bees. *Journal of Sleep Research* 13:145–152.

Sauer, S., et al. 2003. The dynamics of sleep-like behaviour in honey bees. *Journal of Comparative Physiology A: Neuroethology, Sensory, Neurological, and Behavioral Physiology* 189:599–607.

Wcislo, W. T., and S. Tierney. 2009. Behavioural environments and niche construction: The evolution of dim-light foraging in bees. *Biological Reviews of the Cambridge Philosophical Society* 84:19–37.

Question 4: Do any bees forage at night?

Warrant, E. J. 2004. Vision in the dimmest habitat on earth. *Journal of Comparative Physiology A: Neuroethology, Sensory, Neural, and Behavioral Physiology* 190:765–789.

————. 2008. Seeing in the dark: Vision and visual behavior in nocturnal bees and wasps. *Journal of Experimental Biology* 211:1737–1746.

Wcislo, W. T., et al. 2004. The evolution of nocturnal behavior in sweat bees, *Megalopta genalis* and *M. ecuadoria* (Hymenoptera: Halictidae): An escape from competitors and enemies? *Biological Journal of the Linnean Society* 83:377–387.

Question 5: How does the queen control the hive?

Beekman, M., and B. P. Oldroyd. 2006. When workers disunite: Intraspecific parasitism by eusocial bees. *Annual Review of Entomology* 53:19–37.

Beggs, K. T., et al. 2007. Queen pheromone modulates brain dopamine function in worker honey bees. *Proceedings of the National Academy of Sciences* 104:2460–2464.

Butler, C. G., R. K. Callow, and N. C. Johnston. 1962. The isolation and synthesis of queen substance, 9-oxodec-trans-2-enoic acid, a honeybee pheromone. *Proceedings of the Royal Society B: Biological Sciences* 155:417–432.

Grozinger, C. M., et al. 2003. Pheromone mediated gene expression in the honey bee brain. *Proceedings of the National Academy of Sciences, U.S.A.* 100, Supplement 2:14519–14525.

Grozinger, C. M., et al. 2007. Genome-wide analysis reveals differences in brain gene expression patterns associated with caste and reproductive status in honey bees (*Apis mellifera*). *Molecular Ecology* 16:4837–4848.

Lattorff, H.M.G., et al. 2007. Control of reproductive dominance by the *thelytoky* gene in honeybees. *Biology Letters* 3:292–295.

Pierce, A. L., L. A. Lewis, and S. S. Schneider. 2007. The use of the vibration signal and worker piping to influence queen behavior during swarming in honey bees, *Apis mellifera*. *Ethology* 113:267–275.

Stark, R. E., et al. 1990. Reproductive competition involving oophagy in the socially nesting bee *Xylocopa sulcatipes*. *Naturwissenschaften* 77:38–40.

Vergoz, V., H. A. Schreurs, and A. R. Mercer. 2007. Queen pheromone blocks aversive learning in young worker bees. *Science* 317:384–386.

Whitfield, C. W., A. Cziko, and G. E. Robinson. 2003. Gene expression profiles in the brain predict behavior in individual honey bees. *Science* 302:296–299.

Wilson, E. O., and W. H. Bossert. 1963. Chemical communication among animals. *Recent Progress in Hormone Research* 19:673–716.

Question 7: What is honeycomb?

Hales proves hexagonal honeycomb conjecture. On the Web site Frank Morgan's Math Chat. See http://www.maa.org/features/mathchat/mathchat_6_17_99.html. Accessed April 5, 2008.

Pratt, S. C. 2000. Gravity-independent orientation of honeycomb cells. *Naturwissenschaften* 87:33–35.

———. 2004. Collective control of the timing and type of comb construction by honey bees (*Apis mellifera*). *Apidologie* 35:193–205.

Question 8: What is propolis?

Bankova, V. 2005. Recent trends and important developments in propolis research. *Evidence-Based Complementary and Alternative Medicine* 2:29–32.

Question 10: Is there a yearly cycle in the hive?

Bonney, R. E. 1990. *Hive management.* Pownal, VT: Garden Way Publishing.

Chapter 6: Bees at Work

Question 1: Why do bees pollinate flowers?

Harder, L. D., and J. D. Thomson. 1989. Evolutionary options for maximizing pollen dispersal of animal-pollinated plants. *American Naturalist* 133:323–344.

Westerkamp, C. 1996. Pollen in bee-flower relations: Some considerations on melittophily. *Botanica Acta* 109:325–332.

Westerkamp, C., and R.Claßen-Bockhoff. 2007. Bilabiate flowers: The ultimate response to bees? *Annals of Botany* 100:361–374.

Question 3: How do flowers attract bees?

Barth, F. G. 1991. *Insects and flowers: The biology of a partnership.* Princeton, NJ: Princeton University Press.

Kevan, P. G. 1975. Sun-tracking solar furnaces in high arctic flowers: Significance for pollination and insects. *Science* 189:723–726.

Ledford, H. 2007. Plant biology: The flower of seduction. *Nature* 445:816–817.

Seymour, R. S., C. R. White, and M. Gibernau. 2003. Environmental biology: Heat reward for insect pollinators. *Nature* 426:243–244.

Question 4: Are there any flowers that bees prefer or avoid?

Biesmeijer, J.C., et al. 1999. Niche differentiation in nectar-collecting stingless bees: The influence of morphology, floral choice and interference competition. *Ecological Entomology* 24:380–388.

Human, H., and S. W. Nicholson. 2008. Flower structure and nectar availability in *Aloe greatheadii* var. *davyana:* An evaluation of a winter nectar source for honeybees. *International Journal of Plant Science* 169:263–269.

Petanidou, T. Temporal patterns of resource selection in plant-pollinator communities of the Mediterranean: What do they really tell us? On the Web site University of the Agean. See http://www.cc.uoa.gr/biology/medecos/presentations/Friday/1s/Petanidou.pdf. Accessed June 27, 2008.

Rhoades, D. F., and J. C. Bergdahl. 1981. Adaptive significance of toxic nectar. *American Naturalist* 117:798–803.

Romero, G. A., and C. E. Nelson. 1986. Sexual dimorphism in *Catasetum* orchids: Forcible pollen emplacement and male flower competition. *Science* 232:1538–1540.

Seeley, T. D. 1986. Social forging by honeybees: How colonies allocate foragers among patches of flowers. *Behavioral Ecology and Sociobiology* 19:343–354.

———. 1996. *The wisdom of the hive: The social physiology of honey.* Cambridge, MA: Harvard University Press.

Stephenson, A. G. 1981. Toxic nectar deters nectar thieves of *Catalpa speciosa. American Midland Naturalist* 105:381–383.

Willmer, P. G. 1986. Foraging patterns and water balance: Problems of optimization for a xerophilic bee, *Chalicodoma sicula. Journal of Animal Ecology* 55:941–962.

Question 6: How much weight in pollen can a bee carry?

Escaravage, N., and J. Wagner. 2004. Pollination effectiveness and pollen dispersal in a *Rhododendron ferrugineum* (Ericaceae) population. *Plant Biology* 6:606–615.

Giovanetti, M., and E. Lasso. 2005. Body size, loading capacity and rate of reproduction in the communal bee *Andrena agilissima* (Hymenoptera; Andrenidae). *Apidologie* 36:439–447.

Marshall, A., T. Michaelson-Yeates, and I. Williams. How busy are bees—modelling the pollination of clover. On the Web site Iger Innovations.

See http://www.iger.bbsrc.ac.uk/Publications/Innovations/In99/ch3 .pdf19. Accessed July 28, 2008.

Nicholson, S. W., and H. Human. 2008. Bees get a head start on honey production. *Biology Letters* 4:299–301.

Romero, G. A., and C. E. Nelson. 1986. Sexual dimorphism in *Catasetum* orchids: Forcible pollen emplacement and male flower competition. *Science* 232:1538–1540.

Question 7: Do bees ever stop collecting nectar?

Giovanetti, M., and E. Lasso. 2005. Body size, loading capacity and rate of reproduction in the communal bee *Andrena agilissima* (Hymenoptera; Andrenidae). *Apidologie* 36:439–447.

Question 9: How do bees make beeswax?

Brown, R. H. 1981. *Beeswax,* 2nd ed. Burrowbridge, Somerset, U.K.: Bee Books New and Old.

Loveridge, J. Honeycomb. On the Web site The Chemistry of Bees. See http://www.chemsoc.org/exemplarchem/entries/2001/loveridge/ index-page4.html. Accessed April 3, 2008.

Question 10: How is beeswax used in different cultures?

Congdon, L.O.K. 1985. Water-casting concave-convex wax models for cire perdue bronze mirrors. *American Journal of Archaeology* 89:511–515.

Crane, E. 1983. *The archaeology of beekeeping.* Ithaca, NY: Cornell University Press.

———. 1999. *The world history of beekeeping and honey hunting.* New York: Routledge.

Ransome, H. M. 1937. *The sacred bee in ancient times and folklore.* London: Butler and Tanner, Ltd.

Teale, E. W. 1940. *The golden throng: A book about bees.* Binghamton, NY: Vail-Ballou Press.

Chapter 7: Honey

Question 1: What is honey?

Bishop, H. 2005. *Robbing the bees: A biography of honey.* New York: Free Press.

Cutting, K. F. Honey and contemporary wound care: An overview. On the Web site Ostomy Wound Management. See http://www.o-wm .com/article/8058. Accessed April 6, 2008.

Ellis, H. 2004. *Sweetness and light: The mysterious history of the honeybee.* New York: Harmony Books.

Molan, P. C. 2006. The evidence supporting the use of honey as a wound dressing. *Lower Extremity Wounds* 5:40–54.

Subrahmanyam, M. 2006. Honey, a nutritious food and valuable medicine. *Science India* 2:6–8.

————. 2007. Topical application of honey for burn wound treatment—an overview. *Annals of Burns and Fire Disasters* 20:137–139.

Question 2: How does nectar become honey?

Human, H., and S. W. Nicolson. 2008. Flower structure and nectar availability in *Aloe greatheadii* var. *davyana:* An evaluation of a winter nectar source for honeybees. *International Journal of Plant Science* 169:263–269.

Nicolson, S. W., and H. Human. 2008. Bees get a head start on honey production. *Biology Letters* 4:299–301.

Question 4: Is honey good for you?

Frankel, S., G. E. Robinson, and M. R. Berenbaum. 1998. Antioxidant capacity and correlated characteristics of 14 unifloral honeys. *Journal of Apicultural Research* 37:27–31.

Gheldof, N., and N. J. Engeseth. 2002. Antioxidant capacity of honeys from various floral sources based on the determination of oxygen radical absorbance capacity and inhibition of in vitro lipoprotein oxidation in human serum samples. *Journal of Agriculture and Food Chemistry* 50:3050–3055.

Gheldof, N., X. H. Wang, and N. J. Engeseth. 2002. Identification and quantification of antioxidant components of honeys from various floral sources. *Journal of Agriculture and Food Chemistry* 50:5870–5877.

Gheldof, N., et al. 2003. Buckwheat honey increases serum antioxidant capacity in humans. *Journal of Agriculture and Food Chemistry* 51:1500–1505.

Kreider, R. B., et al. 2002. Honey: An alternative sports gel. *Strength and Conditioning Journal* 24:50–51.

Moore, O. S., et al. 2001. Systematic review of the use of honey as a wound dressing. *BMC Complementary and Alternative Medicine* 1:2.

Paul, I. M., et al. 2007. Effect of honey, dextromethorphan, and no treatment on nocturnal cough and sleep quality for coughing children and their parents. *Archives of Pediatric Adolescent Medicine* 161:1140–1146.

Subrahmanyam, M. 1991. Topical application of honey in treatment of burns. *British Journal of Surgery* 78:497–498.

———. Topical application of honey for burn wound treatment—an overview. On the Web site Annals of burns and fire disaster. See http://www.medbc.com/annals/review/vol_20/num_3/text/vol20 n3p137.asp. Accessed September 13, 2008.

Vitusek, S. 1979. Nutrition aspects of athletic performance. II: Is more better? *Nutrition Today* 14:10–17.

Zeina, B., B. I. Zohra, and S. al-Assad. 1997. The effects of honey on Leishmania parasites: An in vitro study. *Tropical Doctor* 27, Supplement 1:36–38.

Question 8: Can honey be toxic to humans?

Deinzer, M. L., et al. 1977. Pyrrolizidine alkaloids: Their occurrence in honey from tansy ragwort (*Senecio jacobaea L.*). *Science* 195:497–499.

Gunduz, A. 2006. Mad honey poisoning. *American Journal of Emergency Medicine* 24:595–598.

Gunduz, A., et al. 2007. Wild flowers and mad honey. *Wilderness and Environmental Medicine* 18:69–71.

Question 9: What is mead?

Crane, E. 1999. *The world history of beekeeping and honey hunting.* London, UK: Taylor & Francis.

Gayre, R., and C. Papazian. 1986. *Brewing mead: Wassail! In Mazers of Mead.* Boulder, CO: Brewers Publications.

Morse, R. A. *Making mead honey wine: History, recipes, methods and equipment.* Cheshire, CT: Wicwas Press, LLC.

Ransome, H. M. 1937. *The sacred bee in ancient times and folklore.* London: Butler and Tanner, Ltd.

Schramm, K. 2003. *The compleat meadmaker: Home production of honey wine from your first batch to award-winning fruit and herb variations.* Boulder, CO: Brewers Publications.

Chapter 8: Bees on the Move

Question 4: How does the swarm locate its new home?

Beekman, M., R. L. Fathke, and T. D. Seeley. 2006. How does an informed minority of scouts guide a honey bee swarm as it flies to its new home? *Animal Behaviour* 71:161–171.

Question 6: Do bees migrate?

Oldroyd, B. P., and S. Wongsiri. 2006. *Asian honey bees: Biology, conservation and human interactions.* Cambridge, MA: Harvard University Press.

Whynott, D. 1991. *Following the bloom: Across America with the migratory beekeepers.* New York: Tarcher/Penguin.

Question 7: How far do bees fly?

von Frisch, K. 1967. *The dance language and orientation of bees.* Cambridge, MA: Harvard University Press.

Question 10: How do foraging bees find their way home?

Dyer, F. C. 1994. Spatial cognition and navigation in insects. In *Behavioral Mechanisms in Evolutionary Ecology,* ed. L. Real, 66–98. Chicago: University of Chicago Press.

———. 1996. Spatial memory and navigation by honeybees on the scale of the foraging range. *Journal of Experimental Biology* 199:147–154.

Dyer, F. C., N. A. Berry, and A. S. Richard. 1993. Honey bee spatial memory: Use of route-based memories after displacement. *Animal Behavior* 45:1028–1030.

Dyer, F. C., and J. A. Dickinson. 1996. Sun-compass learning in insects: Representation in a simple mind. *Current Directions in Psychological Science* 5:67–72.

Giurfa, M., and E. A. Capaldi. 1999. Vectors, routes and maps: New findings about navigation in insects. *Trends in Neurosciences* 22:237–242.

Menzel, R., et al. 1990. Dominance of celestial cues over landmarks disproves map-like orientation in honey bees. *Naturforsch* 45:723–726.

Question 12: What is playflight behavior?

Becker, L. 1958. Untersuchungen über das Heimfindevermögen der Beinen. *Zeitschrift fuer Vergleichende Physiologie* 41:1–25.

Capaldi, E. A., et al. 2000. Ontogeny of orientation flight in the honeybee revealed by harmonic radar. *Nature* 403:537–540.

Capaldi, E. A., and F. C. Dyer, 1999. The role of orientation flights on homing performance in honey bees. *Journal of Experimental Biology* 202:1655–1666.

Vollbehr, J. 1975. Zur Orientierung junger Honigbienen bei ihrem ersten Orientierungs⁻ug Zool. *Zoologische Jahrbuecher Abteilung fuer Allgemeine Zoologie und Physiologie der Tiere* 79:33–69.

von Frisch, K. 1967. *The dance language and orientation of bees.* Cambridge, MA: Harvard University Press.

Chapter 9: Bee Stings and Other Defenses

Question 4: Why do bees sting?

Beshers, S. N., and J. H. Fewell. 2001. Models of division of labor in social insects. *Annual Review of Entomology* 46:413–440.

Question 5: Do killer bees really exist?

Winston, M. L. 1992. *Killer bees: The Africanized honey bee in the Americas.* Cambridge, MA: Harvard University Press.

Question 7: How do stingless bees defend themselves?

Ono, M., I. Okada, and M. Sasaki. 1987. Heat production by balling in the Japanese honeybee, *Apis cerana japonica* as a defensive behavior against the hornet, *Vespa simillima xanthoptera* (Hymenoptera: Vespidae). *Experientia* 43:1031–1032.

Papachristoforou, A., et al. 1995. Unusual thermal defence by a honeybee against mass attack by hornets. *Nature* 377:334–336.

Papachristoforou, A., et al. 2007. Smothered to death: Hornets asphyxiated by honeybees. *Current Biology* 17:R795-R796.

Roubik, D. W., B. H. Smith, and R. G. Carlson. 1987. Formic acid in caustic cephalic secretions of stingless bee, *Oxytrigona* (Hymenoptera: Apidae). *Journal of Chemical Ecology* 13:1079–1086.

Voeller, D., and J. Nieh. On the Web site Analysis of stingless bee aggression. See http://www-biology.ucsd.edu/labs/nieh/TeachingBee/eds _stingless.htm. Accessed July 23, 2008.

Weaver, N., and E. C. Weaver. 1981. Beekeeping with the stingless bee *Melipona beecheii* by the Yucatan Maya. *Bee World* 62:7–18.

Question 9: What is bee venom?

Simics, M. 1996. Changes in bee venom therapy. *American Bee Journal* 136:107–109.

Question 10: Does collecting venom kill the bees?

Bee venom collector devices. On the Web site Apitronic Services. See http://www.beevenom.com/collectordevices.htm#COLL. Accessed April 5, 2008.

Simics, M. 1993. *A review of bee venom collecting and more.* Richmond, B.C., Canada: Apitronic Services.

————. 1995. Bee venom collection—past, present and future. *American Bee Journal* 135: 489–491.

Chapter 10: Dangers to Bees

Question 2: How do bees survive harsh weather?

Fahrenholz, L., I. Lamprecht, and B. Schricker. 1989. Thermal investigations of a honey bee colony: Thermoregulation of the hive during summer and winter and heat production of members of different bee castes. *Journal of Comparative Physiology B: Biochemical, Systemic, and Environmental Physiology* 159:551–560.

Jones, J. C., et al. 2005. The effects of rearing temperature on developmental stability and learning and memory in honey bees (*Apis mellifera*). *Journal of Comparative Physiology A: Neuroethology, Sensory, Neurological, and Behavioral Physiology* 191:1121–1129.

Question 3: What parasites and insects prey on bees?

Fry, C. H., K. Fry, and A. Harris. 1992. *Kingfishers, bee-eaters and rollers.* Princeton, NJ: Princeton University Press.

Harrison, J. F., et al. 2001. Mite not make it home: Tracheal mites reduce the safety margin for oxygen delivery of flying honeybees. *Journal of Experimental Biology* 204:805–814.

Question 4: Which other animals prey on bees?

Attenborough, D. 1998. *The life of birds.* Princeton, NJ: Princeton University Press.

Dean, W.R.J., and I.A.W. MacDonald. 1981. A review of African birds feeding in association with mammals. *Ostrich* 52:135–155.

Short, L. L., and J.F.M. Horne. 2002. Family Indicatoridae (Honeyguides). In *Handbook of the birds of the world,* ed. J. del Hoyo, A. Elliott, and J. Sargatal, 274–295. Barcelona, Spain: Lynx Edicions.

Question 7: How are bee diseases spread?

Stow, A., et al. 2007. Antimicrobial defenses increase with sociality in bees. *Biology Letters* 3:422–424.

Question 10: What is colony collapse disorder?

Berenbaum, M. R. 2007. Colony collapse disorder and pollinator decline. Testimony before the Subcommittee on Horticulture and Organic Agriculture, Committee on Agriculture, U.S. House of Representatives. March 29, 2007.

Colony Collapse Disorder Working Group, Mid Atlantic Apiculture Research Education Consortium. See http://maarec.cas.psu.edu/. Accessed December 22, 2008.

Cox-Foster, D. L., et al. 2007. A metagenomic survey of microbes in honey bee colony collapse disorder. *Science* 318:283–287.

National Academy of Sciences. 2006. *State of pollinators in North America.* Washington, DC: National Academies Press.

Chapter 11: Beekeeping

Question 4: What is a bee skep?

Horn, T. 2006. *Bees in America: How the honey bee shaped a nation.* Lexington: University Press of Kentucky.

Sidebar 1: The Honey Bee Colony as Superorganism

Amdam, G., and S. C. Seehuus. 2006. Order, disorder, and death: Lessons from a superorganism. *Advanced Cancer Research* 95:31–60.

Dawkins, R. 1976. *The selfish gene.* New York: Oxford University Press.

Hölldobler, B., and E. O. Wilson. 2009. *The superorganism: The beauty, elegance, and strangeness of insect societies.* New York: W. W. Norton and Company.

———. 1990. *The ants.* Cambridge, MA: Belknap Press.

Sidebar 2: Metamorphosis

Davies, H., and C. A. Butler. 2008. *Do butterflies bite?* New Brunswick, NJ: Rutgers University Press.

Sidebar 3: Epigenetics

Amdam, G. V., and R. E. Page. 2005. Intergenerational transfers may have decoupled physiological and chronological age in a eusocial insect. *Aging Research Reviews* 4:398–408.

Barchuk, A. R., et al. 2007. Molecular determinants of caste differentiation in the highly eusocial honeybee *Apis mellifera. BMC Developmental Biology* 7:70.

Drapeau, M. D., et al. 2006. Evolution of the yellow/major royal jelly protein family and the emergence of social behavior in honey bees. *Genome Research* 16:1385–1394.

Edgell, T. C., and C. J. Neufeld. 2008. Experimental evidence for latent developmental plasticity: Intertidal whelks respond to a native but not an introduced predator. *Biology Letters* 4:385–387.

Huang, Z., and G. E. Robinson. 1996. Regulation of honey bee division of labor by colony age demography. *Behavioral Ecology and Sociobiology* 39:147–158.

Kucharski, R., et al. 2008. Nutritional control of reproductive status in honeybees via DNA methylation. *Science* 319:1827–1830.

Lattorff, H.M.G., et al. Control of reproductive dominance by the *thelytoky* gene in honeybees. *Biology Letters* 3:292–295.

Omholt, S. W., and G. V. Amdam. 2004. Epigenetic regulation of aging in honeybee workers. *Science of Aging Knowledge Environment* 26:pe28.

Whitfield, C. W., A. Cziko, and G. E. Robinson. 2003. Gene expression profiles in the brain predict behavior in individual honey bees. *Science* 302:296–299.

Sidebar 4: Bees' Learning Abilities

Dedej, S., and K. S. Delaplane. 2005. Net energetic advantage drives honey bees *(Apis mellifera L)* to nectar larceny in *Vaccinium ashei Reade. Behavioral Ecology and Sociobiology* 57:398–403.

Farina, W. M., C. Gruter, and P. C. Diaz. 2005. Social learning of floral odours inside the honeybee hive. *Proceeds of the Royal Society of London: Biological Sciences* 272:1923–1928.

Gil, M., and R. J. DeMarco. 2005. Olifactory learning by means of trophallaxis in *Apis mellifera. Journal of Experimental Biology* 208:671–680.

Giurfa, M., et al. 1996. Detection of coloured stimuli by honeybees: Minimum visual angles and receptor specific contrasts. *Journal of Comparative Physiology A: Neuroethology, Sensory, Neural, and Behavioral Physiology* 178:699–709.

Giurfa, M., et al. 2001. The concepts of sameness and difference in an insect. *Nature* 410:930–933.

Leadbeater, E., and L. Chittka. 2005. A new mode of information transfer in forging bumblebees? *Current Biology* 15:R447–R448.

———. 2007. The dynamics of social learning in an insect model, the bumblebee *(Bombus terrestris). Behavioral Ecology and Sociobiology* 61:1789–1796.

———. 2008. Social transmission of nectar-robbing behaviour in bumble bees. *Proceedings of the Royal Society B: Biological Sciences* 275:1669–1674.

Saleh, N., et al. 2006. Facultative use of the repellent scent mark in foraging bumblebees. *Animal Behavior* 71:847–854.

Saleh, N., and L. Chittka. 2006. The importance of experience in the interpretation of conspecific chemical signals. *Behavioral Ecology and Sociobiology* 61:215–220.

Stach, S., J. Bernard, and M. Giurfa. 2004. Local-feature assembling in visual pattern recognition and generalization in honeybees. *Nature* 429:758–761.

Worden, B. D., and D. R. Papaj. 2005. Flower choice copying in bumble-bees. *Biology Letters* 1:504–507.

Sidebar 6: Pollination

Branson, A., et al. 1993. *The illustrated encyclopedia of mammals.* New York: Andromeda Oxford.

Case Study 3: Honey possums and wildflowers. On the Web site American Association for Employment in Education. See http://www.aaee .org.au/docs/WAbugs/cs3.pdf. Accessed April 6, 2008.

Del Hoyo, J., A. Elliot, and D. Christie. 2006. *Handbook of the birds of the world.* Vol. 12. New York: Lynx Editions.

Driskell, A. C., and L. Christidis. 2004. Phylogeny and evolution of the Australo-Papuan honeyeaters (Passeriformes, Meliphagidae). *Molecular Phylogenetics and Evolution* 31:943–960.

Gomez, J. M., et al. Spatial variation in selection on corolla shape in a generalist plant is promoted by the preference patterns of its local pollinators. *Proceedings of the Royal Society B: Biological Sciences* 275:2241–2249.

Hoehn, P., et al. 2008. Functional group diversity of bee pollinators increases crop yield. *Proceedings of the Royal Society B: Biological Sciences* 275:2283–2291.

Huang, Z. Y., and G. E. Robinson. 1996. Regulation of honey bee division of labor by colony age demography. *Behavioral Ecology and Sociobiology* 39:147–158.

Thorp, R. 1979. Structural, behavioral, and physiological adaptations of bees (Apoidea) for collecting pollen. *Annals of the Missouri Botanical Garden* 66:788–812.

Sidebar 7: How Do Plants Attract Bees for Pollination?

Benitez-Vieyra, S., et al. 2007. How to look like a mallow: Evidence of floral mimicry between Turneraceae and Malvaceae. *Proceedings of the Royal Society B: Biological Sciences* 274: 2239–2248.

Dyer, A. G., et al. 2006. Bees associate warmth with floral colour. *Nature* 422–423:525.

Sapir, Y., A. Shmida, and G. Ne'eman. 2005. Pollination of *Oncocyclus* irises (*Iris:* Iridaceae) by night-sheltering male bees. *Plant Biology* 7:417–424.

———. 2006. Morning floral heat as a reward to the pollinators of the Oncocyclus irises. *Oecologia* 147:53–59.

Schemske, D. W., and H. D. Bradshaw. 1999. Pollinator preference and the evolution of floral traits in monkeyflowers (*Mimulus*). *Proceedings of the National Academy of Sciences* 96:11910–11915.

Schiestl, F. P., et al. 1999. Orchid pollination by sexual swindle. *Nature* 399:421.

Schiestl, F. P., and S. Cozzolino. 2008. Evolution of sexual mimicry in the orchid subtribe Orchidinae: The role of preadaptations in the attraction of male bees as pollinators. *BMC Evolutionary Biology* 8:27.

Sidebar 8: Bees and Honey in Judiasm

Encyclopaedia Judaica. 2nd ed. Vol. 1. Jerusalem, Israel: Keter Publishing House, Ltd.

Sidebar 10: Honey in Islam

Ali, A. 1988. *Al-Qur'an: A contemporary translation.* Princeton, NJ: Princeton University Press.

Sidebar 11: Honey Hunting in Rock Art

Crane, E. 1999. *The world history of beekeeping and honey hunting.* London, UK: Taylor & Francis.

Sidebar 12: Mayan Beekeeping

Ransome, H. M. 1986. *The sacred bee in ancient times and folklore.* London: Butler & Tanner LTD.

Sidebar 13: The Great Pollinator Research Project in New York City

The great pollinator project. On the Web site NYC Beewatchers. See www.nycbeewatchers.org. Accessed September 6, 2008.

Making it work: The bee team. On the Web site *New York Times.* See http://query.nytimes.com/gst/fullpage.html?res=9800E5DF143FF9 33A25754C0A962958260. Accessed September 6, 2008.

Matteson, K. C., J. S. Ascher, and G. A. Langellotto. 2008. Bee richness and abundance in New York City urban gardens. *Annals of the Entomological Society of America* 101:140–150.

Pollinator partnership. See http://www.pollinator.org. Accessed September 6, 2008.

Sidebar 14: Stingless Bees

Heard, T. 1999. The role of stingless bees in crop pollination. *Annual Review of Entomology* 44:183–206.

Roubik, D. W. 1989.*Ecology and natural history of tropical bees.* Cambridge, UK: Cambridge University Press.

Royal Mayan bee. On the Web site Bees for Development Organization. See http://www.beesfordevelopment.org/info/info/stingless/royal-mayan-bee.shtml. Accessed August 8, 2008.

Slaa, E. J., et.al. 2006. Stingless bees in applied pollination. *Apidologie* 37:293–315.

Sidebar 15: The Story of Brother Adam

Bee keeping at Buckfast. On the Web site of The Buckfast Abbey. See http://www.buckfast.org.uk/site.php?use=bees. Accessed August 14, 2008.

Bill, L. 1989. *For the love of bees: The story of Brother Adam of Buckfast Abbey.* Devon, U.K.: David & Charles.

The Buckfast breeding program. On the Web site beesource.com. See http://www.beesource.com/pov/osterlund/proceedings.htm. Accessed August 14, 2008.

The monk and the honey bee. On the Web site Paul Jungels. See http://www.beekeeping.com/articles/us/adam.htm. Accessed August 14, 2008.

Index

About the Authors

Elizabeth Capaldi Evans, PhD, is an associate professor of biology and animal behavior at Bucknell University in Lewisburg, Pennsylvania. Trained in zoology, ecology, and evolutionary biology, her research interests focus on the behavior, ecology, and neuroethology (the study of the nervous system as it functions during natural behavior) of insects, with a specific focus on bees. Honey bees are the main focus of her work, but she also conducts research on a variety of other bee species. Her studies have been published in a wide variety of scientific journals, including the multidisciplinary journal *Nature,* the *Annual Review of Psychology,* and the bee-focused *Journal of the Kansas Entomological Society.* Evans regularly speaks to local beekeeping clubs and organizations about her research and about other issues of importance to the beekeeping community.

Carol A. Butler, PhD, is the co-author of the Rutgers University Press question and answer series that includes *Do Butterflies Bite?* (2008), *Do Bats Drink Blood?* (2009), *Do Hummingbirds Hum?* (2010) and *How Fast Can a Falcon Dive?* (2010). She also co-authored *Salt Marshes: A Natural and Unnatural History* (2009) and *The Divorce Mediation Answer Book* (1999). She is a psychoanalyst and a mediator in private practice in New York City, an adjunct assistant professor at New York University, and a docent at the American Museum of Natural History.